NXT

NXT Cryptocurrency

Publisher: Valeur d'histoire

Director: apenzl

Writers: apenzl, abctc, Dave Pearce, Cassius, Lionel Jeannerat, RubénBC, Bas Wisselink, Daniel M. Ryan, Roberto Capodieci, Robert Bold.

Editor: Robert Bold

Translators: Seccour, Jose

Design: Shee Visual Design

With special support from:

- Nxt Foundation

- The community members of Nxt

Second edition

Printed by lulu.com

ISBN 978-2-9700947-9-1

NXT

unsurpassable blockchain solutions

NXT Cryptocurrency

Discover the link of
SurpriseAlias

NXT Cryptocurrency

TABLE OF CONTENTS

 NXT Cryptocurrency

NXT
preface

PREFACE

Written by: apenzl

The publication of this book was successfully crowdfunded via the Nxt platform in late January 2016,[1] which means that, from conception to delivery, it has been some 9 months in gestation. A long time, especially in the cryptosphere, but unsurprising when you consider that development of the Nxt ecosystem never stops and therefore writing the book has been like chasing a moving target. At the heart of Nxt development is the Nxt core developers' roadmap which has itself evolved, but also ideas about how to improve Nxt are always floating in from the Nxt community, the best of both worlds being realised in code and launched in new NRS releases.

My original intention was to base the publication on a pdf-book, which had been compiled from Nxter.org articles in English, Spanish, Russian and Chinese by members of the Nxt Community for Nxt's 2nd anniversary. Some of those articles are still included in the book. Many have had to be edited and updated, others didn't make it, and as Nxt has evolved, new chapters have had to be written.

The announcement of Nxt 2.0, Ardor, represents a fundamental shift in the developers' focus away from Nxt 1.0, and therefore a natural juncture at which to conclude the book.

And here's the result. You'll get a simplified 'snapshot' of the Nxt

---

1 https://nxter.org/crowdfunding-the-first-book-about-the-nxt-cryptocurrency-platform

ecosystem as of October 2016; an introduction to its genesis and early history, its main features, its community and also some Nxt Services. Much has been tried and much has been developed on the Nxt platform. The services mentioned in the book have been chosen because of their developers' long term dedication to Nxt and the community, and/or the originality of their projects and visions. The book does not cover all use cases for Nxt, as this would be impossible (only the future can reveal the most groundbreaking of them), neither does the book aim to offer an extensive guide to the Nxt Client interface or the Nxt API for developers. Instead it offers a general insight into the versatility of the platform and links to in-depth information.

There is a lot of thanks to be given.

First, to the team behind this publication. Authors and translators of the original pdf.[2] Ludom for his support, nerve and execution of the crowdfunding campaign, and for wanting to publish it. Writers: abctc, Daniel M. Ryan, Lionel Jeannerat, Dave Pearce, Bas Wisselink, RubénBC, Jose, Roberto Capodieci, Zahlen, and more. Robert Bold (known on the Nxt forum as 'oldnbold') for his editing, authoring and proofreading work. Riker and Jean-Luc for fact-checking the technical articles. Shee for cover design and her help to set up all the content. *Hash* and Ideenfrishe for the Nxt logo and for the Nxt global corporate design[3] (big up, Michael). And the full Nxter. org Team for your patience and for updating, tweeting, discussing, keeping our site alive and running while I was intensively working

---

2 https://nxter.org/nxt-2nd-birthday
3 https://nxtforum.org/nxt-promotion/a-global-corporate-design

on finishing the book. Special thanks to Rubén, Jose, yassin, marenkar, and MrCluster87.

To all backers of the book, who bought into the crowdfunding campaign by ordering books in advance, trusting us not to run away with the funds and actually to publish the book as promised.

And then, of course, cheers to BCNext for his initial ideas and Nxt codebase, but even more than that to current Nxt lead developer Jean-Luc and the rest of the developers, who have continuously contributed core code to Nxt and made the advancement of blockchain technology possible: Come-from-Beyond. WesleyH, Scripter-Ron, Holgerd77, Kushti, Jones, Mr V, Petko, Mess, ChuckOne, Riker, testdruif. A hearty thanks also to testers and third-party developers who have played around with the Nxt API, created user friendly services, alternative clients, blockchain explorers, development tools, new business models, and have inspired us all.

The Nxt Community: the lurkers (silent investors), and all active contributors and participants in the ongoing discussion on the forums, be they users, asset issuers, MS currency issuers, DGS users or merchants, or working for Nxt behind the scenes. The uniqueness and solidarity of this community, through bear- and bull-markets, depression and enthusiasm, still looking out for each other[4], earning trust, raging at each other at times but still cooperating on successfully solving very difficult tasks in just fragments of time... this community keeps blowing my mind. And I'm grateful to be a

---

4 https://nxtforum.org/general-discussion/need-help-from-nxt-community-selling-assets

part of it.

The Nxt feature descriptions in this book are based on NRS change-logs, the Nxt Bitbucket repository, Nxtwiki.org, Nxter.org articles, videos, Nxtchat.slack- and Nxtforum.org posts, i.e. they are based on the thoughts and work of the active Nxt Community. To mention just a few contributors; QBTC, blackyblack, Tosch110, NxtSwe, evildave, Damelon, Zahlen, Daedelus, farl4bit, slothbag, chanc3r, brangdon, verymuchso, durerus, wolffang, Cassius, Jones, CryptKeeper, forkedchain, RickyJames, BitcoinPaul, chanc3r, ThomasVeil, VanBreuk, jl777, MarcDeMesel, 2Kool4Skewl, BrooklynBTC, rlh, emoneyRu, Anon138, capodieci..... You get the idea. This is not even close to being an exhaustive list - thanks goes to everyone who has contributed their thoughts and skills over the years!

A 'Thank You' must also be given to the initial stakeholders who invested in the Nxt IPO, in late 2013. They believed in BCNext's initial idea and saw what Nxt could become. Contrary to the often repeated criticism about Nxt's 'unfair' distribution method, it could be argued that BCNext's initial distribution was precisely what saved Nxt, but it has certainly been a double-edged sword.

Some of the early investors have actively written code, others have contributed to the development of Nxt with donations to the hard working Nxters, understanding that that would be a wise way to protect their investment in Nxt. In addition, non-spending whales like 4747...888[5] have an important role in the ecosystem, contribu-

---

[5] 4747...888 owns: https://www.mynxt.info/account/4747512364439223888

ting with a constantly forging stake of 50 million NXT, thereby lowering the network's vulnerability to attacks since the very beginning. Another example of a 'nice whale' is Megalodon, who stepped forward with an economic incentive for smaller Nxt accounts to forge and set up more nodes by donating 5M NXT to a "forging lottery"[6].

„A world with money can never be perfect", was BCNext's short answer to the community[7], when asked about his distribution. And it's true, the generous behavior of SOME whales has certainly not been the behaviour of all whales. The initial distribution has ridden us like a mare, as other whales have continually dumped, every time the price of NXT rose – they cashed out. I do not blame them - but I give them no thanks. Investors who bought in later have been through hard times, as the early whales controlled the Nxt market at large for a long period of time, and scared off others from looking into the tech.

In December 2013 I was celebrating Christmas with my family. I was there, and I sat still, ate, laughed with them, and I left. I ran down to my home office, again and again that evening, ripped open my laptop and refreshed The Nxt Monsterthread[8]. I was, at the time, an unsuccesful altcoin trader and had recently discovered Nxt on Coinmarketcap.com[9].

Nxt was under attack. I did not then have the knowledge needed

---

6 https://nxter.org/the-forging-bounty-lottery-campaign-will-pay-5-million-in-rewards-to-forgers-and-nxt-nodes
7 https://bitcointalk.org/index.php?topic=345619.msg4383169#msg4383169
8 https://bitcointalk.org/index.php?topic=345619.msg4102598#msg4102598
9 Website which ranks small and major cryptocurrencies and crypto assets by their market cap.

to help, and my stake was of a laughable size, but I couldn't leave the thread: what went on here was amazing. The coolness of the actors, the positive spirit in spite of the situation just hooked me. I watched it happen; fast analysis, and action: fight back. No-one was asking for donations, but set up nodes, bought VPS's, set up more nodes, offered help to those who didn't know how to do it, fought back to save and secure the newly launched Nxt ledger. Only later did I realise that most in the thread were legendary members of that Bitcoin forum.

The Nxt protocol is not all that's going to leave traces into the future. The community's cooperation, the blend, the social experiment has also proven itself. The time has come for more people to learn about, and build upon, our supreme platform, use the features, and make progress. Give life to new secure, disruptive, decentralised blockchain applications with Nxt.

To me, this book is the documentation of a very intense journey, and the beginning of a new era. What has been achieved thus far by the Nxt Community is absolutely astonishing.

Welcome to the past and the future, put into words by the Nxt Community. The future will not be centralised. It will be you. Enjoy, and take part. We're right here.

/apenzl

NXT
introduction

 **NXT** Cryptocurrency

INTRODUCTION

Written by: abctc[1], apenzl

At its launch in 2013, Nxt was ostentatiously dubbed: 'The Descendant of Bitcoin'.

Before going into detail about Nxt, it's helpful to remind ourselves why Bitcoin, which was invented by an individual or group known as 'Satoshi Nakamoto', is considered a work of genius.

It's not just because Bitcoin is the world's first decentralised payment system with its own integrated currency. More than that, it is a decentralized mechanism to secure the cooperation of a theoretically limitless number of people who, by following pre-specified rules (a protocol), are able to create and validate a public ledger of transactions. That was indeed a huge, truly revolutionary invention.

For those who aren't familiar with Satoshi's ground-breaking innovation, decentralised (p2p) collaboration already existed in the form of peer-to-peer file sharing technology. The music-sharing application, Napster[2], was one early adopter and popularised the technology. The perfect example of that is a torrent, a more advanced version of the technology being the BitTorrent protocol[3]. The main problem with a torrent system is that it's not protected from cheaters. Moreover, a lot of people only want to download torrent files, but not to share them.

---

1 https://nxter.org/ru/что-делает-nxt-криптоплатформой-второго
2 https://en.wikipedia.org/wiki/Napster
3 https://en.wikipedia.org/wiki/BitTorrent

Satoshi took a crucial further step – he found a way to make all the p2p participants strictly follow the rules and, in doing so, protect themselves from cheaters and thieves. In effect he had solved the 'Byzantine Generals' problem"[4].

"Peer-to-peer (P2P) computing or networking is a distributed application architecture that partitions tasks or work loads between peers. Peers make a portion of their resources directly available to other network participants, without the need for central coordination by servers or stable hosts. Peers are equally privileged, equipotent participants in the application. They are said to form a peer-to-peer network of nodes."[5]

Satoshi's solution is based on the so-called 'Proof-of-Work' concept, whereby the cost incurred by any aspiring fraudster would exceed any benefits he would get. His invention was: the Bitcoin Protocol[6].

The advantages of Bitcoin are many. You get full control over your own money, transactions take place between users directly, without an intermediary, you can transfer Bitcoins across borders with very low fees 24/7, and all transactions are immutably secured by network nodes and recorded in a public distributed ledger; anyone can check their validity.

There are though, also inherent disadvantages to the design, in particular: the system is not scalable as the blockchain size keeps growing and nodes need to host the full chain; the huge waste of

4 https://en.wikipedia.org/wiki/Byzantine_fault_tolerance
5 Source: https://en.wikipedia.org/wiki/Peer-to-peer
6 https://bitcoin.org/bitcoin.pdf (Bitcoin: A Peer-To-Peer Electronic Cash System)

electricity because thousands and thousands of specialised mining rigs have to run day and night competing against each other - all for nothing unless they hit a block. And increasing mining difficulty has made it impossible for average users to participate as they can't afford the expensive specialised hardware. This has lead to centralisation of mining power in mining pools and professionally driven mining-farms[7].

The creator of Nxt, building on Satoshi's ideas, sketched out his vision of a distributed cryptographically secure blockchain platform, comprising not only a digital payment system, but a wide range of built-in services and the capacity for third party developers to add their own applications, all fully secured by the Nxt Proof-of-Stake (PoS) protocol[8]. In the PoS model, network security is governed by peers having a stake in the network. 'Forging' NXT (the Nxt equivalent to the 'mining' of Bitcoins) is energy efficient, as the software can run on small devices like a laptop computer or even a Raspberry Pi without exhausting it.

> *"The incentives provided by Nxt's algorithm do not promote centralization in the same way that Proof of Work algorithms do, and data shows that the Nxt network has remained highly decentralized since its inception. Nxt's unique algorithm does not depend on any implementation of the coin age concept used by other PoS cryptocurrencies, and is resistant to so-called Nothing at Stake attacks."[9]*

---

7 http://www.coindesk.com/bitcoin-nodes-need
8 https://nxter.org/bcnexts-nxt
9 Source: https://nxtwiki.org/wiki/Whitepaper:Nxt

While the Average Joe may still be confused as to what Bitcoin is, for the rest of us the hype moved from Bitcoin to Blockchain, from Blockchain to Blockchain 2.0, and now it is focused on 'smart contracts'. A smart contract is, basically, a conditional transaction.

"A smart contract is a piece of code which is stored on a blockchain, triggered by blockchain transactions, and which reads and writes data in that blockchain's database."

~ Gideon Greenspan[10]

Nxt does not use smart contracts, but 'smart transactions'. When talking about smart contracts, the best known example is the Ethereum project[11]. On Ethereum, smart contracts materialize as snippets of code (a script), which define the inputs, mechanism, and outputs of a given transaction. Once the code is written, it is sent to the blockchain and is executed upon specific triggers. Ethereum smart contracts are executed on all the nodes, and their final output is validated in the same manner as any other blockchain transaction. This has unfortunately proven to be a potentially dangerous approach path[12].

With Nxt's smart transactions, the code which is executed is actual software that runs in the node server; Nxt transactions do not require any script processing or transaction input/output processing on the part of network nodes; scripts are already embedded. When a user wants to express their opinion at a poll, purchase an item

---

10 http://www.the-blockchain.com/2016/04/12/beware-of-the-impossible-smart-contract
11 https://www.ethereum.org
12 http://www.inc.com/minda-zetlin/cryptocurrency-crowdfunding-experiment-ends-in-disaster-when-hackers-steal-53-m.html

in the marketplace, or sell some stocks, the transaction the user submits contains only the parameters necessary for the transaction, and the ID of the functionality they want to use, keeping the consensus of the majority of the nodes as the absolute proof that the output, saved in the next block, is the genuine result of that transaction. By leveraging these primitive Nxt transaction types, Nxt can be seen as an agile, base-layer protocol upon which developers without much prior knowledge in the cryptocurrency field can easily create a limitless range of secure decentralised services, applications, and even other currencies[13].

"Bitcoin has proven that a peer-to-peer electronic cash system can indeed work and fulfil payments processing without requiring trust or a central mint. However, for an entire electronic economy to be based on a fully decentralised, peer-to-peer solution, it must be able to do the following: process transactions quickly, efficiently and securely; provide incentives for people to participate in securing the network; scale globally with a minimal resource footprint; offer a range of basic transaction types that launch cryptocurrencies past the core feature of a payment system alone; provide an agile architecture that facilitates the addition of new core features and allows for the creation and deployment of advanced decentralised applications; be able to run on a broad range of devices, including mobile ones, and Nxt satisfies all of these requirements".

~ Lior Yaffe[14]

---

13 Another difference between smart transactions and smart contracts is that a computer application has tenfold more power and possibilities, compared to a script interpreted in a virtual machine.
14 Advanced Concepts in Blockchain Design (Lior Yaffe, July 2016): https://youtu.be/soHe4UMyCCk

"The potential benefits of the blockchain are more than just economic – they extend into political, humanitarian, social and scientific domains. The blockchain is in a position to become the fifth disruptive computing paradigm after mainframes, PCs, the Internet, and mobile/social networking."

~ Melaine Swan[15]

At the time of writing, Nxt has enjoyed almost 3 years of stable operation. Its design and core functionality has been proven in practice, in addition to being subjected to code review by independent experts in the cryptocurrency field, as well as hackers, who have tried to exploit it unsuccessfully. Nxt's wide range of functionality, coupled with its proven, secure, modular and developer friendly design means that it will probably continue leading, or at the very least keep pace with, the cutting edge of independent, permissionless blockchain technology, and it will therefore always remain one of the world's foremost cryptocurrency platforms, making it the true 'Descendant of Bitcoin'. What may have been an ostentatious statement in 2013, has in fact turned out to be accurate.

15 Blockchain – Blueprint for a New Economy (Melaine Swan, ISBN-13: 978-1491920497)

The Genesis:

the miss america of
alternate cryptocurrencies

 NXT Cryptocurrency

THE GENESIS: THE MISS AMERICA OF ALTER-NATE CRYPTOCURRENCIES

Written by: Daniel M. Ryan[1]

September 27th, 2013. That was the day when a mysterious fellow with the username „BCNext" signed up for Bitcointalk[2]. The next day, he posted an announcement that would change the direction of cryptocurrencies forever.

The announcement was for a cryptocurrency which he called "Nxt". Not only was it to be coded from scratch but it was also to be coded in a language that was completely different from the standard C++. Nxt was to be programmed in Java[3].

Moreover, Nxt had a new wallet system called a 'brain wallet'. The typical cryptocurrency has a file in the user's computer, typically named 'wallet.dat.' (...) The brainwallet system, in contradistinction, has no definite file in which the Nxt holder's coins are stored. They're essentially stored in the databases of all the peers. So, there's no explicit file target for a hacker to copy. In addition to this security model, the brainwallet emulates Java's „write once, run anywhere" philosophy. With a Nxt brainwallet, you can „deposit once, access anywhere."

---

1 Originally posted on August 28, 2014. http://www.enterstageright.com/archive/articles/0814/cryptocurrp5.htm. Printed with permission.
2 https://bitcointalk.org/index.php?action=profile;u=152600
3 https://java.com

But back then in late September of 2013, Nxt had not even been developed. Some Bitcointalk members, seeing or suffering from the scams afoot in the IPO circuit, decided that there would only be one robbery. That robbery would be of the naïfs who sent BCNext some Bitcoin, and the robber would be none other than BCNext. Yes: during the pre-sale phase, which actually lasted until November 18th, there were more than a few Bitcointalk members who decided that Nxt was a plain scam. Joining them were more than a few scoffers, and some rather clever people who opined that BCNext would send the Bitcoin he collected on a 'round-trip' so as to make his pre-sale seem more popular than it was and to get a big stake in Nxt for himself. But some believed in BCNext and his vision for a completely new cryptocurrency with Proof-of-Stake 'forging' to secure the network, registrable aliases, instant messages, a completely new infrastructure... and an inbuilt asset exchange. That asset exchange would capture the holy grail of the crypto world: so-called 'colored coins' that could be used to represent an outside asset. Seventy-three of those believers became the initial stakeholders of Nxt: BCNext raised 21 Bitcoins from them. The genesis block that would create all the Nxt was to contain one billion new coins.

When the presale was closed a few hours after midnight Eastern time on November 18th, only ninety-nine accounts were entitled to receive NXT from the pre-sale. One Bitcointalk member, arguably, had had the presale window slammed shut on his fingers. His complaints, plus a simmering under-the-surface hostility in Bitcointalk that had been aggravated by the sudden riches and steaminess of

Altcoin Boom Town, would prove to be a fateful course changer in the entire alternate cryptocurrency world. It didn't help that BCNext decided to vanish and communicate to his stakeholders via a spokesman named Come-From-Beyond.

The last time BCNext visited Bitcointalk, under that username, was November 8th 2013. Since then, he has communicated indirectly. The reason, so he said, was because he was afraid of being tracked down by the CIA or suchlike because they would believe that he had developed a new Silk Road[4]. He later revealed indirectly that he was involved in crypto under another name and he hinted that he might be back some day under yet another username with a completely different project. Despite his conspiratorial-minded exit statement, the parallel with Bitcoin's original developer Satoshi Nakamoto was quite evident. His supporters and fans found it easy to believe that he was in the same rank as Satoshi Nakamoto. Some even wondered if he was Satoshi Nakamoto. The unimpressed, naturally, didn't think anything of the sort. They were inclined to make far less flattering comparisons.

In BCNext's last message, he said that Nxt would be released in early January. In actuality, he generated the blockchain-starting genesis block less than thirty-six hours after he halted the pre-sale. And a little later, on November 20th, Come-from-Beyond unveiled the web address of a 'bootstrap node' that stakeholders could use to access their allocations of Nxt.

---

4 https://en.wikipedia.org/wiki/Silk_Road_(marketplace)

The unveiling proceeded to be a little more complicated because some stakeholders did not supply valid identification or even iden-tify themselves at all. So the earlier genesis block was voided and a new one was regenerated. In the meantime, in the early afternoon of November 20th, Come-From-Beyond offered to sell 1 million NXT for 1 BTC, or 100 satoshis per NXT. Someone else quoted a price ten times higher. That got two complaints, one somewhat easygoing, about Come-From-Beyond quoting a price that was (in actuality) almost fifty times what he paid. In response, Come-From-Beyond said that 100 satoshis would prove to be a real bargain by late January of 2014. Another early adopter 2Kool4Skewl, averred the same thing. 2Kool4Skewl was evidently quite convincing: thir-ty-five minutes after his endorsement, Come-From-Beyond rescin-ded the offer.

No-one complained heatedly, but that 'genesis offer' did show (perhaps unintentionally) a somewhat mercenary attitude. On the other hand, there were seeds of generosity sprouting too. One IPO stakeholder said he was going to give away 1000 NXT to his friends, and Come-From-Beyond pledged to set up a 'faucet:' a website where a visitor could get a small allocation of free coins. Faucets were nothing new – Bitcoin had had them for a long time – but it did show a side in the earliest-adopter community that was the opposite of rapacious. Within a day, another first adopter - neer.g - pledged to donate 4 million of his NXT to a giveaway fund. But before that pledge, another IPOer offered 1 million of his own for that same 1 BTC. Showing that he was serious, 2Kool4Skewl quickly offered to buy them all. „NXT @ 0.000001 btc [100 satoshis] is an investment I can't afford to miss." He meant what he said. On November 21st, mid-afternoon Eastern Time, yet another first adopter named Noitev posted, „I'm selling 15 Million NXT to 2Kool4Skewl for 15 BTC....Since there is no client yet, I will need an escrow..." Soon after that, 2Kool4Skewl confirmed that he would be sending his 15 BTC to an escrower. The 'genesis exchange' had taken place only half a week after the pre-sale had been closed.

On late afternoon on the 21st, Come-From-Beyond explained the reason for the hurry-up: BCNext wanted the core group of Nxters to run things in his stead. But because of the advance in schedule, the first version of Nxt would only be basic. The entrancing features in his original proposals[5] would be disabled for a long time. Anyone lurking in the thread, wondering if something was fishy with Nxt, had another item to add to the fishiness list. At the time though no-one piped up.

In retrospect, even though the most likely motive was BCNext deciding to remove himself from the scrutiny of the authorities that he thought were watching him, his decision was a stroke of managerial genius. By being the 'Leader who Refuses to Lead', by being the 'Sleeping King', BCNext left a vacuum that was soon filled by a whole crew of really solid programmer talent. One of them, Jean-Luc at Bitcointalk and Jean-Luc-Picard in the Nxt neighbourhood, became the official chief developer for Nxt and the maintainer of the official Nxt repository[6] on Bitbucket. As of the time of this writing, there is a whole confederacy of developers for Nxt. They're all hard at work

---

5 https://bitcointalk.org/index.php?topic=303898
6 https://bitbucket.org/JeanLucPicard/nxt/commits/all

extending its functionality and/or providing third-party services overlaying Nxt itself. Some have gone beyond even BCNext's vision.

Of course, with respect to that masterstroke, there was some luck involved. The Leader who Refuses To Lead can create a vacuum that's filled by indecision and infighting, as seems to be the case with Gentoo Linux. But BCNext's vision provided a rallying touchstone, and – to be frank – he was lucky that he had captivated top-notch talent.

The total talent in play for Nxt rivals only Bitcoin's. In fact, Nxt is the only alternate cryptocurrency with a collection of core programming talent that rivals a high-tech start-up. Ethereum, the latest hot offering in the coded-from-scratch second-generation cryptocurrency sector, claims to have a comparable suite of genius, but it's not scheduled to launch until January of 2015. Unlike Nxt, Ethereum has generated a lot of publicity and its pre-sale has called forth tens of thousands of Bitcoins for its Ethers. Their haul has been three orders of magnitude greater than Nxt's 21. Ethereum claims to be far more innovative than Nxt, but the time between its announcement and its scheduled release will be more than eleven months[7].

After the new genesis block was pruned of unidentified or unidentifiable stakeholders, Come-from-Beyond announced late morning Eastern Time November 22nd that it was time for the remaining stakeholders to claim their coins. The pruned genesis block allocated 49,875,751 NXT for the maximum 1 BTC investment for an implied

---

7 Editors note: Ethereum launched on July 30 2015.

price of about 2.005 satoshis per NXT. Remember, there already was a formal commitment by two parties – both the seller and the buyer - to exchange 15 million NXT at almost fifty times the pre-sale price.

Without anyone quite knowing it at the time, a real fuse had been lit – even though the buyer, the aforementioned 2Kool4Skewl, was an openly eager demander (of fifteen million more than his initial IPO stake) at that price. Only a slight hint of the fuse now inaudibly hissing came from the seller, Noitev, who suggested to his committed buyer: „Be sure not to hog them all, they'll go up more and be better if you distribute them to a lot of people."

Just a cautionary note, expressed in a casual and even friendly tone. A cautionary note, posted at suppertime Eastern Time on November 22nd, 2013. Any newbie lurking at that time would see nothing more than a reminder about the need for wider distribution. Nothing more than that.

The jubilation on late November 22nd was mixed with confusion and some fright. Come-from-Beyond reminded everyone that BCNext had posted a link to a Desktop Nxt client on October 29th, although it was recommended that the IPO recipients register their accounts at the bootstrap Web client set up by Come-from-Beyond. That registration was part of a procedure for each stakeholder to claim his or her coins: in the final iteration, the step-by-step instruction comprised twelve full steps. Come-from-Beyond had to explain the procedure for running a Nxt, Nxt clone or Nxt offshoot wallet: fire up the client - then necessitating opening up a command prompt window, changing its directory to the Nxt files' folder and typing in" java -cp Nxt.zip Nxt" – and then opening up a new browser window. Once the command-prompt part of the wallet had fully booted up and signalled that Nxt was running, the user had to put the address "http://localhost:7875" in the opened browser. The browser, after getting the user's passphrase, would open up the interactive Java-script wallet. Or at least, that's the way it should have worked. After one eager IPOer started up the command-line client and got the message „Nxt 0.1.5 started", his client started throwing exception errors. Come-from-Beyond had to advise, „Ur version is not compatible with mine. Use it just to generate an account id. Later we all get the most recent version."

It's not hard to imagine curious altcoin-vet lurkers in the thread starting to snicker. Yet another launch. Yet another messy launch. Yet another launch where the 'groundbreaking' tech goes haywire. But this mess included something new: having to straighten out clashes between different and network-incompatible versions of the clients. BCNext expressed a real distaste for cloners, heartily seconded by his growing circle of core Nxters, so he announced through Come-from-Beyond that Nxt's source code would remain secret until early January: more-or-less the same date as his origi-nally-promised release. The Nxt version that entered crypto history as the first with source code proved to be 0.4.7. Jean-Luc Picard, for historical reasons, still offers it for download[8]. But the code, now open source, was not exactly cloneable for real. Again through

---

8 https://bitbucket.org/JeanLucPicard/nxt-public/src

Come-from-Beyond, BCNext explained that he deliberately introduced three subtle but serious security flaws in the source code for 0.4.7. Those flaws would be revealed in three months' time if no-one had found them by then.

Come-from-Beyond, shrewdly, made a contest out of it. The discoverer of flaw #1 would win 1,000 NXT. For the discoverer of flaw #2, 10,000 NXT. For the diligent and insightful discoverer of flaw #3, 100,000 NXT. This announcement spawned a Bitcointalk thread[9] that ended up growing to 69 pages. And got a lot of Bitcointalk members poking through the source code, and getting an inadvertent self-education on how Nxt's innards worked. Some of these people would take their learning and join the high-powered developer community, now comprised of well over twenty developers. As for the rewards, they were all claimed before the contest was over – and in order. More than a month passed when the only one still open was the frustratingly subtle flaw #3. The winner, Evil-Knievel, got awarded the bounty on March 22nd - twelve days before the contest was to end and the flaws revealed.

After fielding a fair number of questions and help requests, Come-from-Beyond announced that the Nxt network would be fully operational as of noon GMT November 24th. And then he went back to fielding questions and help requests - and noting that Nxt required more than 256 megabytes of memory allocated to the Java runtime environment else it had a habit of crashing. He also included a pre-warning with a list of account numbers that would be sent Nxt

9 https://bitcointalk.org/index.php?topic=397183.0

come go-time. He told those first adopters to check their details carefully, because once Nxt was a go the sends would be irreversible. Less than an hour and a half later, the first hint of the hissing fuse surfaced in a somewhat angry complaint from one of the IPO stakeholders. Unlike most of the others, he had not followed the progress of Nxt. He said that claiming what was his had become a lot more complicated than what BCNext had originally promised. „That's pretty much work for an investment <100$". Little did he know, not having followed the thread, that at the first-trade price of 100 satoshis his „<100$" already had an implied value of four figures.

As launch time approached, Come-from-Beyond was still busy fielding help request after help request. Some of the lurkers in the thread were obviously less than charmed by this seeming donkey derby. Shortly after the go-time, the first criticism threads appeared, claiming that Nxt was flawed, rickety and with unplanned security vulnerabilities. Ironically, that stroke-of-genius Sleeping King talent drive was already on the job: by early January, five different wallet clients were available. But those complaints, numerous as they were, were truly weak sauce to the fury that exploded over a completely different issue. Nxt was not just the pioneer of completely Bitcoin-independent second-generation cryptocurrencies. It was also the pioneer, through being the #1 punching bag, for an outpouring of economic populism that shot through the ostensibly libertarian altcoin world.

Completely unintentionally, and only as the #1 'plutocrat' villain,

Nxt also induced a serious flirtation with cryptocurrency socialism. The first one-shot trading price of 100 satoshis served as a precedent for the first phase of price discovery in Nxt's official trading thread[10]. That precedent price was also close to the starting price of trading on the first day Nxt was listed on its first 'real' exchange, Dgex: that day being November 29th 2013. It was at that point that the lit fuse entered the dynamite sticks. But the explosion didn't come until November had turned into December, the month where Dgex's price discovery revealed that Nxt had become another get-rich-quick altcoin.

December 25th, 2013, was a holly-jolly Christmas for the original still-holding stakeholders who had paid an implied price of only 2.005 satoshis for their NXT. On December 25th at 12 AM, NXT traded at 7,884 satoshis for more than a 393,000% gain in Bitcoin terms in three months or less. A hypothetical punter who bought 1 BTC for two hundred and fifty dollars on Halloween 2013, and threw it into NXT shortly afterwards, could (only conceivably) have sold his stake on the beginning of Christmas morn for more than 3900 Bitcoins. And then, turn and (more realistically) unload that 3900 BTC for US$ for more than US$700 per Bitcoin. Had this impossibly lucky person done precisely that, said luck-struck fellow would have turned that $250 into approximately two point seven three million dollars. For the first time in crypto history, a hot alt had made at least one lucky holder an outright millionaire on one single starter Bitcoin. For the first time in cryptocurrency history, an alt posted a percentage gain that was in the range of Bitcoin's itself – but in a jarringly compressed time frame. What took Bitcoin three

10 https://bitcointalk.org/index.php?topic=345336.0

full years to rack up, Nxt racked up in three months.

Even more strikingly, Nxt's subsequent performance was more or less a wide-ranging side channel. Nxt has pretty much held its value after its Boom Town stampede ended. A buyer of NXT on December 25th had lots of chance to exit with either a teeny profit or greater. The canny developer-recruitment tactics and the check-out-the-innards publicity stunt, secured enough top-notch talent to keep Nxt innovations churning out more or less continually.

BCNext's original vision has mostly been realized, and several side services has been added that hadn't even been dreamed of. Because of that top-notch talent, Nxters have a serious shot at beating the Ethereum dream team by implementing all of Ethereum's future features before Ethereum's launch. The only exceptions would be Ethereum features downchecked by Nxt's Jean-Luc Picard as being too risky, or too ill-thought-through, for Nxt.

Yes, it is admittedly true that there were a few days in late November when Nxt could have been justifiably dubbed 'Klutzerella.' But as the subsequent eight months demonstrated, particularly the months where NXT held most of its value, Nxt is the altcoin world's answer to Miss America. Indeed, for the original stakeholders who held, and even for the early buyers who relieved the selling stakeholders of their NXT at an almost 50-bagger in Bitcoin terms, Christmas 2013 was a very merry Christmas. 2Kool4Skewl, that eager IPO participant who bought 15 million more at 50X his IPO price, had been bang-on right in his forecast.

But for the ones who had missed out - there she was, Miss Nxt-erica. By her mere presence, she had unintentionally elicited a very unhappy and soon-to-be-rancorous New Year...

NXT

its history and potential

 NXT Cryptocurrency

NXT:
ITS HISTORY AND POTENTIAL

Written by: Lionel 'Ludom' Jeannerat[1].

> *"It was a bright cold day in April, and the clocks were striking thirteen".*
>
> ~ Nxt Genesis account

As a veteran of the Nxt platform and its ecosystem, I think I can provide an interesting perspective for investors, entrepreneurs and the merely curious. Moreover, on the occasion of this publication, I thought it was my duty to make my contribution to help explain what Nxt is.

I hope that my account, non-exhaustive and necessarily subjective as it is, will be of interest. As I wasn't involved at the time when 'BC-Next' announced the Nxt project, I will not go into detail regarding the beginnings of Nxt. Nevertheless, the forum exchanges from that period[2] are worth reading.

The gestation

After a subscription period of more than 40 days, BCNext (via Co-me-from-Beyond) announced that 21 BTC had been sent to him

---

1 Originally posted November 3, 2015: https://nxter.org/fr/joyeux-anniversaire-nxt-deux-annees-deja-1-sur-3. Translated by Seccour.
2 https://bitcointalk.org/index.php?topic=303898.0

by around seventy anonymous investors. The point of the subscription was not to raise a lot of money. The objective was to justify an initial distribution.

This element is essential because the Nxt program, in its code, does not allow for a distribution of the NXT token over time. All NXTs were created exclusively in the first block, and any generation of additional tokens is impossible. Frequently cited as a problem, the fact that the entire NXT token supply was distributed all at once is for me actually one of the greatest strengths of Nxt.

We have no evidence that the initial investors were as many as advertised, some may have subscribed several times. But so what? In my opinion, BCNext isn't accountable for anything and his distribution choice was a matter entirely for him. Nxt was designed as a 100% Proof-of-Stake blockchain, and the distribution therefore had to be made on the first block.

The first steps

Nxt was a unique project of its kind: 100% proof-of-stake and a completely new code, written in Java. At that time, Bitcoin had made a surge to $1,000 per token. The crypto-enthusiasts had generally made money (me included). But 'the exclusivity of Bitcoin' was a problem for many. Altcoins flourished, each bringing its own set of more or less interesting novelties. The market was very liquid and sophisticated investors (or the lucky ones) and market manipulators could make money easily. Nxt wasn't an exception, but its dynamic was different from all the Bitcoin forks that flourished at that time. The Nxt community crystallized around a popular thread[3] (as its number of pages can attest) on Bitcointalk. Personally, I was very strongly attracted to Nxt because it solved certain critical problems affecting Bitcoin and its PoW clones: the ever-increasing hashrate and therefore cost of mining, the consequent huge waste of electricity (representing a massive loss of productive investment value to the ecosystem as well as being very damaging to the environment) and the concentration of mining power in fewer and fewer hands leading to centralisation of the network, which is bad for both the security and 'governance' of the Bitcoin network. In addition to that, what BCNext wanted to create was a financial transaction platform, not merely a cryptocurrency payment system, but the 'Descendant of Bitcoin'.

I began to follow the thread carefully. And I was seduced. It must be said that Nxt was the first crypto 2.0 project and this attracted a lot of interest from those who expected more of crypto than could be provided by Bitcoin, limited (as it is) by its inherently limited capacity for change. At the time, I got the impression that discussions were relatively high level. The range of subjects discussed was broad and prominent among them was the exciting potential of a crypto 2.0 platform. For over four months, this topic was the primary focus of the entire community. At that time, personalities started to emerge alongside the pioneers and developers Jean-Luc and Come-from-Beyond, including amongst others: jl777, Damelon, allwelder, Salsacz, far14web, 2Kool4Skewl ... No doubt I've forgotten some of them. Some people left, others are still there. But the

3 https://bitcointalk.org/index.php?topic=345619.0

sense of community cohesion that was created then still remains today.

This single Bitcointalk thread was inconvenient and the community wanted to migrate to somewhere more conducive to the productive exchange of information and ideas and so it was that, after some deliberation, the Nxt community took up residence at nxtforum.org[4].

Taking shape

Moving on from the bitcointalk forum, the community has continued its dynamic exchange of news, opinion and counter-opinion. The transition went very well and the use of a clean, mostly troll-free forum elevated the level of debate even higher. The community clearly went into high gear. Version 1.0 of Nxt arrived and some projects were beginning to materialize. I also think that it was during this period that community cohesion became more established.

In my opinion it was clear from the beginning that Nxt showed great promise and needed only to mature for its full potential to be recognised. However back in early 2014 many people, still conditioned by the Bitcoin example, had a more limited perspective on what was involved. So it was that a lot of Nxters at the time were in effect only speculators, rather than long term investors, and saw the NXT token as merely being a 'new currency of the future'. Projects, the community, everything was still in its infancy. But the idea

4 https://nxter.org/nxt-newsletter-archieve/nxt-newsletter-7

of a cryptographically secure, decentralized 'economic' platform rather than simply a cryptocurrency based payment system was beginning to develop in the community.

The asset market

It was in this favorable environment that the Asset Exchange was launched. Some community members understood the potential of this new feature right from the start[5]. One of the first was jl777 (James). The projects he had been considering since Nxt first started could finally be brought to life. James back then claimed to be „just a simple c programmer" but his plans went beyond simple technological innovation. An experienced financial trader, he was the only one who understood how to use the Nxt platform to set up a robust 'Keiretsu' type financial structure (i.e. a conglomeration of projects linked together by cross-shareholdings).

James created a large number of assets associated with his projects: MGW (MultiGateWay, a distributed mechanism to transfer Bitcoin and altcoins to/from the Nxt blockchain, where they can be traded or kept), InstantDEX (a decentralized trading system), and he also explored other types of assets, including: jl777hodl (a portfolio of assets) and Nxtventure (an asset that paid dividends in the form of other assets, representing projects in which it invested). By interlacing his assets, his financial system became a complex construction which may be hard to grasp at first, but was actually well thought out[6].

5 https://nxter.org/nxt-newsletter-ae-special
6 Learn more about jl777's assets here: https://nxter.org/assethub

To a certain extent of course James was experimenting a bit, like the sorcerer's apprentice (exploring the full potential of the new technology). Indeed many of us were experimenting - I even launched some assets (MIC and pvhistoire) myself; but don't search for them, they have no value anymore.

The euphoria helped to boost the market. The success was very important. Nxt was the first of its kind. There were, of course, also the inevitable scams. And the biggest at that time was Cointropolis. CoinTropolis_JustaBit was a smooth talker who had managed to take the lead in the promotion of Nxt. Like a car seller, he succeeded in generating lots of interest and creating an excitement around Nxt by promising big news. As a result of his promotional activity, combined with the successful launch of the Asset Exchange, the NXT price reached its (to date) all time high during the 2014 PayExpo in London[7]. But JustaBit's promises were false, he was a dishonest and unscrupulous speculator. Not content with his profit from NXT trading, he took the opportunity to raise funds by issuing what turned out to be scam assets. He even managed to steal some Bitcoins directly from other Nxt community members. Unsurprisingly he disappeared shortly afterwards and has not been heard of since.

This period, from late spring to summer 2014, was a true El Dorado. Trading volumes were very high. For my part, I took the opportunity to make some profits with my savings. I regularly made some good trades and managed to avoid falling for any of the scams then

---

[7] https://nxtforum.org/payexpo-(london-june-11-12-2014)/payexpo-london-11-12-june

being run, sometimes because I saw them for what they were and other times purely by chance.

A return to normal

Gradually, the euphoria moderated. Trading volumes nevertheless remained high and the Asset Exchange consolidated its success. Moreover, the community was beginning to understand how the new tools at their disposal worked and the implications they had for the development of the Nxt ecosystem. The relative madness gave way to an equally relative wisdom. It is difficult to summarize this long period covering the second half of 2014. A lot of things happened, some of the more interesting of which I discuss below.

The main exchange website of that time was bter.com. In August of that year they were robbed of 51 million NXT. This event reads like a bizarre detective story. But the most striking aspect was how it tested the resilience and cohesion of the Nxt Community. The Nxt lead developer, Jean-Luc, proposed clearing the transactions from the theft with a 'roll back'. Under his proposal, those Nxters who wished to do so could use an alternative version of NRS (the Nxt program) which reorganized the blocks and removed the transactions tainted by the theft. There was a vigorous debate[8]. Many Nxters were holding NXT on bter.com and were scared they might lose out. But finally, after some reflection, only a few Nxters adopted the alternative NRS. The roll back didn't happen, and Nxt survived with its credibility intact, and the community was strengt-

---

[8] https://nxtforum.org/news-and-announcements/forgers-have-been-faced-with-a-choice

hened[9]. After all, bter.com had only themselves to blame for their incompetence. They have suffered another hack since then, so seemingly have learned nothing...

The inherent weakness of central exchanges like bter.com opened the Nxt community's eyes to the need for a better solution. At the same time jl777 was finalizing the first ever semi-decentralized exchange system: the NXT MultiGateWay, which made it possible to transfer Bitcoins and other altcoins to the Nxt blockchain and exchange them directly within the platform. Fully decentralised trading, yet deposits and withdrawals required external processing, performed by three synchronised independent MGW servers, running multi-sig. This MultiGateWay, although in beta, was one of the first functional projects that fully used the Nxt API to add functionality to Nxt through third party software. It established James as someone who kept his promises. And in Autumn, James launched his great project: SuperNET[10] - in the process raising nearly 5800 BTC to fund the development[11].

Basically, SuperNet would allow James to unify all his projects (and assets) under one flag while expanding collaboration with other projects and other blockchains. Because yes, James broke a real taboo at the time by proposing the idea of different crypto-communities collaborating together to help support each other's cryptocurrencies for the mutual benefit of all.

---

9 http://cointelegraph.com/news/interview-with-nxts-bas-wisselink-and-vericoins-patrick-nosker-the-bter-hack-the-future-and-when-is-it-okay-to-change-history
10 https://nxter.org/meet-james-jl777-nxtinside-supernet
11 https://bitcointalk.org/index.php?topic=762346.0

The Nxt core developers were also hard at work. Later in 2015, the first truly decentralized marketplace in history was launched. So far the Nxt Marketplace has had limited success, as sellers from outside the community have been reluctant to offer their products on the platform, and the Nxt community just isn't large enough. I think this extraordinary feature, among others, was ahead of its time, which is why it hasn't yet enjoyed the success it certainly deserves.

Crossing of the desert

2015 was a difficult year for the crypto-currency market, Nxt was no exception. The price of the NXT token continued to decline. At the beginning of the year, the symbolic price of 5000 satoshis was crossed. Then came the slow and irretrievable falling to 2500 at the time of writing. During the year, NXT was ejected from the top 10 of cryptocurrency marketcap.

Nxt is now no longer the only crypto 2.0 platform, and our competitors are very well funded. Nxt has proven what can be done and has paved the way for our competitors.

I often say that the price of NXT tokens doesn't matter, but I must admit that it's still a cause for concern. Not least as regards the effect it has had on the community's morale. Seeing a steady decline in the value of ones investments tests the strongest of hands. The enthusiasm of the first year did not carry forward to the next. More disturbing to me, the number of transactions (which was ever increasing in 2014) fell in 2015. Moving from an average of 6000 transactions per day beginning in 2015 to about 1,500: Nxt is less used in 2015 than in 2014.

The main reason is a decrease in the use of the Asset Exchange. Assets change hands less often, and the good opportunities have become more scarce. It seems to me that 2015 was the year when many of the short-term speculators left Nxt - it had been their 'day trading' that had accounted for much of the trading volume in 2014. Today the investors who remain are mostly interested in the long-term. This seems to be reflected by the investment trend in the Asset Exchange towards assets offering dividends rather than purely speculative assets. In 2015 we've seen an increasing number of serious assets paying substantial dividends to their owners, yet the Asset Exchange is still being used for fundraising. A recent example that demonstrated the potential of the Nxt platform is Farla Webmedia, a Dutch website company; within hours of its asset being launched it had raised 1.35 million NXT to hire new staff[12]. Although exceptional, this successful campaign is not isolated.

The ecosystem has a solid basis but it suffers from a lack of liquidity. This lack of liquidity is particularly evident from the number of transactions. Nxters have already invested heavily in the ecosystem and expect a return on their investment to 'spend / invest again.'

A metaphor I like to use is that of 'crossing the desert' because it evokes the idea of a powerful and transformative experience - when you survive the desert, you usually come out stronger. And

---

12 https://nxtforum.org/assets-board/(ann)-farla-webmedia-investing-in-a-real-life-company-monthly-dividend

it's certainly the case that during 2015, Nxt has continued to progress.

The development team has not been idle: launching, as they have, the Monetary System in January, and the Voting System in June. Of course, these features have not yet been as successful as the Asset Exchange but they, together with the other new features being added, are all extra strings to the Nxt bow. Through the developers' productivity, Nxt retains its technical edge as a leading decentralised platform.

Nxt - Maturity outlined

Nxt version 1.7 brings exciting new features that complement existing ones like Marketplace, Asset Exchange, Monetary System, etc... With these newly released innovations, Nxt has become a comprehensive platform for decentralized administration, for both private individuals and business. And the further core development and improvement is ongoing. However, whilst the foundations are good, it's not enough. What happens in terms of further development in the coming months will undoubtedly be important, perhaps even decisive as regards the success or failure of Nxt.

Nxt is a unique platform that hosts an even more exceptional ecosystem but, compared with Bitcoin, it's virtually unknown and even within the cryptosphere it's widely misunderstood and misrepresented. Nxt has to carve out its own market niche and to do that its marketing should focus on 'what you can do with Nxt' rather than 'what you can earn by investing in NXT denominated projects or by simply holding the NXT currency'.

Gaining in visibility

The approach of the Tennessee project[13] is interesting in this regard but it's insufficient. A large mobilization of the Nxt Community is essential to attract projects, individuals, and companies to experiment with new ways to use the platform. Everyone can help to raise its profile and its rate of adoption. Nxt doesn't sell currencies, it facilitates others to sell their goods and services. Promoting this message is the way to help Nxt become more visible and therefore grow. For Nxt to clearly stand out from its competitors, a really substantive work should be launched to highlight what Nxt does better than anyone-else (or indeed is the only one to do). This will involve the development of effective and creative uses, as well as explanatory tutorials on how to put them into effect. Media like Nxter Magazine have a crucial role to play here.

Improving the transition process

The steady evolution, if not properly managed, can cause problems for the Nxt ecosystem which must constantly update its servers and adjust its computer programs to accommodate changes. In late October, early November last year, business users and external developers were complaining that some of the changes made by NRS v.1.62 were not backwards compatible and thereby causing

13 See: 'Nxt Foundation - How to market a decentralised open source organisation'

a great deal of unrest in the community, on the market and for the services using Nxt. This is not without negative consequences. Version 1.7 and the many changes it introduced, in preparing for newer versions, created new compatibility issues with external projects. jl777 and others protested loudly about those changes and how they had compromised the development and/or efficient running of their services[14]. Until the problem is properly resolved, it will inevitably reoccur, thereby potentially driving away existing users and putting off new ones.

Unless that happens, this sensitive issue is likely to be the platform users' main bugbear in 2016 and I'm counting on the core developers, the guys from Tennessee, the external developers and the Nxt community to find an acceptable solution for both internal and external developers. The key, of course, is dialogue between all stakeholders. The success of Nxt is no longer only dependent on technology but also on the ecosystem it makes possible.

Conclusion

We are still at the beginning of the adventure and newcomers can invest more cheaply than the original (late) pioneers. The basics are established and strong, but much remains to be done. Personally, I believe that those involved in Nxt (the core and third party developers, the investors, the marketers, writers, translators and supporters - the community as a whole) have proved themselves more than capable of meeting the many and varied challenges that

14 Read more about this in the chapter: 'Nxt 2.0; ARDOR'.

lie ahead. I invite all readers to get onboard the 'Nxt train' to take part in one of the most exciting adventures of our lives. Whether you are rich or poor, it doesn't matter as there's no need to buy anything - ideas and projects are more than sufficient in this decentralised economy. To me, the destination is less important than the journey.

NXT

initializing NRS

 NXT Cryptocurrency

INITIALIZING NRS

Written by: apenzl, Zahlen

"You have to realize that in the land of bitcoin clones, the QT wallet is all they have. All this new stuff is totally new and to go from bitcoinQT to current [Nxt] UI is quite a culture shock, but the nearly universal reaction is, "wow I never knew Nxt was so cool!"

~ jl777, 2014

To start using Nxt, you need to download the client app, which is built into the Nxt core software distribution[1]. This official client provides a simple way to connect to the Nxt network and send transactions, implemented such that your passphrase never leaves your computer (it is never exposed to the network).

Installing the Nxt Client is easy - just download and use an installer from https://nxt.org[2]. There you can also try an online demo of the Nxt Client.

Nxt user accounts are not stored locally. In Nxt, the passphrase[3]

---

1 The NRS (Nxt Reference Software) uses a client-server architecture. The client component is a browser-based, user-friendly interface, referred to as the Nxt Client. The NRS server is a Java application with two interfaces: one for communicating with other servers through the Internet (forming a network of nodes), and one for responding to requests from clients through its API (Application Program Interface).
2 To make sure that the downloaded software is authentic, you can check the SHA256. When new NRS versions are released by the Nxt core development team, they publish a SHA256 hash of the file. If the file has been altered or tampered with, the hash value of the altered file will be completely different. The current version of the client and it's SHA256 can be found in: https://nxtforum.org/nrs-releases.
3 Your private key is derived from your passphrase, and your account number is derived from your public key. You can not change the passphrase for your account later. If you would like to use a different passphrase, you must create a new NXT account and then send your NXT from your old account number to your new one.

determines which account you access, and changing even a single character will lead to a different NXT account. The easiest way to make a strong passphrase is to let the client do it for you. The Nxt Client will generate a passphrase of 12 random words.

You need to type them exactly as you see them: all lowercase characters, with spaces in between words, and no punctuation. Remember: your passphrase is your account. If you lose your passphrase, you will lose access to your account - and everything in it. There is no way to get it back. There are 2^{64} (which is a little under 2 followed by 19 zero's) possible accounts.

The first time you log in to the Nxt Client, you will see a welcome message with your account ID[4] and a public key[5]. The account ID (starting with NXT-...) also appears in the upper left corner of the client. Write down this account ID; it is what other people will use, when they send NXT to you, and it is the ID which will be related to all of your transactions in the Nxt blockchain.

To finalize your account creation, you must announce your public key to the network, because

- A greater level of security will be added to your account. When you have announced your public key, your account is protected 2^{256} against collisions.
- Unless you send a transaction or someone else (a private person or an exchange) sends you a transaction which includes

---

4 https://nxtwiki.org/wiki/RS_Address_Format
5 The "public key" is a string of characters which nodes use to verify your transactions.

your account's public key, your new account will not appear on the blockchain or in any of Nxt's blockchain explorers[6].

To send a transaction, you need NXT. If you own Bitcoins, you can quickly fund your account via Shapeshift[7] from within the Nxt Client or via other cryptocurrency exchanges, like Poloniex, Bittrex.com, or BTC38.com.

If you are new to cryptocurrencies and do not own any, NXT coins can be bought directly from fiat <> NXT exchanges, for example Bitpanda.com or litebit.eu, via bank transfer, SWIFT, SEPA, VISA/Mastercard, etc.[8]

The exchange of your choice will ask you for your account's public key before they transfer your NXTs, and so announce it to the network.

Every time you send something, whether it's NXT coins or some smart transaction, you're adding data to the blockchain. To protect the blockchain against being spammed, any transaction costs a minimum 1 NXT fee. The fee goes to the account that processes the block your transaction is included in (just like how transaction fees go to block finders in Bitcoin).

---

6 A blockchain explorer is a web tool which provides detailed information about blocks, addresses and blockchain transactions.
Examples: https://nxtportal.org, https://www.mynxt.info
7 ShapeShift provides instant Bitcoin and altcoin conversion. Users do not have to create accounts, deposit funds, or provide private personal information.
8 For a full updated list of exchanges, see: https://nxter.org/exchange

Pro tip:

- You can sign transactions offline, if you want optimal security.
- You can earn "forging" fees by running the NRS, or by leasing your account balance to a Nxt "forging hub" if you don't want to run the software 24/7. Your balance will not be locked.
- For testing and development purposes, see: https://nxtwiki.org/wiki/Testnet.

This book will not go into detail with the client interface. You can find further information about how to use the various client features by visiting https://nxtwiki.org or watching the walkthrough tutorial videos on https://nxter.org/tutorials.

NXTER.ORG

nxter magazine

 **NXT** Cryptocurrency

NXTER.ORG
Written by: apenzl[1]

"hello".

Log in to the Nxt Client using this passphrase, and you will log in to an account created by an original stakeholder. You'll see that 10 NXT were transferred to it, and you'll see that the owner sent a message from the account, before the remaining 9 NXT were transferred out. The public message sent was the same as the passphrase itself, a simple "hello".

It's beautiful.

Why? It witnesses the emergence of the brand new technology, Blockchain 2.0. An initial investor tests a new feature, driven by curiosity, or maybe just to check what he actually bought into, and by doing so, by actively testing a feature like "Arbitrary Messaging", leaving a "hello" forever in the blockchain, he becomes an active "Nxter".

Nxter Magazine

When I bought the Nxter.org domain in December 2013, I wanted to create a community service, initially just for Nxters, with which they could follow the development of Nxt without having to spend

---

1 apenzl is the founder of NXTER.ORG, and octopus on the project.

every day hunting down information inside fast moving threads in forums.

I filtered the info, and started writing and publishing the Nxt Newsletter[2]. In the longer term, as I envisaged it, Nxter.org could be turned into a magazine, and not just a news-hub, but also a direct hub to the decentralised Nxt Services[3] which were going to be built on top of Nxt. A way for readers (which of course would soon be every sane individual on Planet Earth), a promotion and marketing tool for Nxt developers, a place to hang out and discuss use cases, and a decentralised Nxt Think Tank.

Lots of people were happy about the Nxter.org initiative, but new writers never stepped forward to help and up until July 2014 it was a fun but exhausting and time-consuming solo performance keeping Nxters in the loop. Even so, traffic to Nxter.org increased, the mailing list grew, not only with committed Nxters, but also with other altcoin enthusiasts, and interestingly, the largest Bitcoin news sites started following us, however they did not themselves publish a single word about Nxt; while the Nxt core developers released version upon version of the Nxt software, quickly increasing its number of groundbreaking features, only readers of Nxter.org or the now various forum threads knew. All larger 'crypto-oriented' news websites published stories only about Bitcoin, Bitcoin entre-preneurs and promising Bitcoin startups (and how many millions of dollars they raised to fund their attempts to develop what Nxt already had working). In other words: They knew about Nxt. They

---

2 https://nxter.org/category/nxt-newsletter-archive
3 Nxt Services is the common name for external applications, plugins, and businesses, that use NXT.

decided to ignore us. They were all heavily invested in BTC.

But then in June 2014, others finally started to get it too;

"Apenzl recently noted that the major crypto news sites seem to ignore NXT. It's like there's a conspiracy of silence. So there was a suggestion to start one of our own. This thread is just to pull together some ideas, find out whether it's viable, and so on - Discovery Phase for Lean lovers. If it's got mileage, great. If not, also fine."

~ Cassius, on nxtforum.org, 2014 [4]

And so it began. Nxter Magazine, with a core team and some 'freelance' article writers and translators, all solidly based in the community. Nxter.org soon expanded into a multilingual news and information site, with each language having its own editor. We now work (and hang out) in nxter.slack, in Basecamp, and on the nxtforum[5]. And occasionally in real life.

"Everyone has at least one field of interest, which is his reason to own or support the Nxt platform. Share it. Write it down. Instead of keeping it to yourself or discussing it among ourselves only - let's spread the word and the visions. Let's get it out there".

~ apenzl, 2014

An asset for the active community

On October 10th, 2014, the asset called NXTP (Nxterpoints) was issu-

---

4 https://nxtforum.org/nxt-promotion/nxt-friendly-crypto-news-site
5 https://nxtforum.org/nxter-org

ed on the Nxt Asset Exchange. NXTP's were to constitute shares in Nxter.org's future profits. There was no IPO.

"All contributions to Nxter.org will be rewarded with Nxter-points (NXTP). These are loyalty points that represents a share of the net profit of Nxter.org. We couldn't find a better way to honor the purpose of the site (decentralisation) or reward the contributing Nxt community. The more you contribute, the more Nxterpoints you'll get [and the more they will be worth]. This to (...) hopefully motivate inactive stakeholders + give new Nxters a way to earn their way in if they want - by writing (get published, get paid campaign[6]), spreading the word or contributing with other skills".

~ apenzl, 2014

The NXTP asset was an experiment; Nxter.org got funded with 240K NXT from the Nxt Marketing Fund Committee[7], which ensured a monthly base dividend to all contributors for 12 months. Part of the experiment was to see if the initiative could become self sufficient within this timeframe[8]. On November 08, 2014, we announced the initiative:

"I'd like to invite you to join us in our efforts @ nxter.org: This is how it will work: http://nxter.org/get-published-get-paid-nxtp/. If this experiment works, it will be a news story in itself. We hope you will con-

---

6 https://nxter.org/get-published-get-paid-nxtp
7 Back when the first investors should claim their stake of NXT, around 9 million NXT was never claimed. On March 7, 2014, the Nxt Community elected 3 funding commit tees with 5 (unpaid) members in each committee to control these unclaimed NXT from the Genesis Block: A TechDev Committee, an Infrastructure Committee, and a Nxt Marketingfund Committee ; https://nxter.org/nxt-funds-committees
8 https://nxtforum.org/marketing-committee/(mc)-nxter-org

tribute. The value of NXTP will be the sum of our work".

~ apenzl[9]

Nxter.org has now been distributing NXTP's and monthly dividends to NXTP holders for more than 2,5 years, and more than 60 Nxters have so far contributed with quality posts and work. Ads give revenue. Articles have been sold. Partnerships are made. Donations have been received as well, in the form of NXT but also asset donations from which all dividends received are passed on to NXTP holders. Every single transaction is traceable on the blockchain. Not a single NXTP has ever been sold by Nxter.org. Every single NXTP found on the Nxt AE market is there, because it has been awarded to someone donating time and skills to the Nxt project in some way, through Nxter.org. The NXTP market price is what it is - people mostly hold their NXTP's for the long term.

Take control

'Blockchain 1.0' coins (like Bitcoin) originally entered into the public consciousness as some form of 'Internet money' whose primary usecase was the trading of illegal goods in dark markets, and as being a high-risk-high-return investment opportunity for risk-seeking investors. That was the story being told and re-told by the mainstream media, and backed by several governments, some of which sent out warnings to their citizens not to trade Bitcoins, while others prohibited local banks from serving customers who transferred money from their bank account to Bitcoin exchanges[10].

9 https://nxtforum.org/general-discussion/write-promote-help-nxt-and-earn-nxtp
10 For examples, see the chapter: 'Fiat is failing - let 'battle' commence?'

'Blockchain 2.0' is now at long last finally getting some attention. First from developers and Bitcoin millionaires, because well funded 2.0 projects, like Ethereum, has spent most of its marketing budget to target those, as they need 3rd party applications developed on top of their blockchain before it becomes useful for ordinary people (and valuable to investors). But also banks, big corporations and governments are beginning to grasp the urgency of understanding the disruptive nature and potential of what has been built and keeps evolving[11].

That is all to the good. But what I think people really need to understand is that *anyone* can use the technology. Anyone can use Nxt, right now. There are video tutorials for all features available on Nxter.org[12]. Do you have a feature or usecase in mind, which is not yet available? Propose it in nxtchat.slack or nxtforum.org[13], or start a blog on nxter.org - pitch your idea and your visions, start a discussion, push forwards. Are you a programmer? Experienced or novice, it's easy to build plugins or apps on top of Nxt, or even to write complicated financial software. Nxter.org has dev tutorials

---

11 Distributed ledger technology: Beyond block chain (https://www.gov.uk/government/news/distributed-ledger-technology-beyond-block-chain), report by the UK Government Chief Scientific Adviser, Sir Mark Walport:
'Government should provide ministerial leadership to ensure that it provides the vision, leadership and the platform for distributed ledger technology within government; this group should consider governance, privacy, security and standards.'
Finextra, in association with IBM: Banking on Blockchain (https://www.ingwb.com/media/1609652/banking-on-blockchain.pdf):
'Blockchain looks set to impact the fabric of the financial services infrastructure. Thinking about that impact and what it might mean, and formulating strategies to respond, is essential. Banks are getting used to reinventing themselves to evolve, and blockchain has the potential to provoke another evolutionary change. (...) Even if it were possible to ignore blockchain, given the hype around it, doing so would be a bad idea, despite the many competing demands on time and budget in the current environment.'
Also read: "Can IBM really make a business out of blockchain?", http://fortune.com/2016/06/28/ibm-blockchain
12 https://nxter.org/tutorials
13 https://nxtforum.org/nxt-improvement-proposals

to get you started[14], nxtwiki.org describes the impressive Nxt API in full, and in the nxtchat you can get in direct contact with experienced Nxt developers who are willing to answer your questions, or even contact the Nxt core development team themselves in the nxtforum. Just jump in and take part in creating the future.

To me, Nxt is a disruptive tool for 'ordinary people' as well as companies and governments. It is free for anyone to use or build on top of, it is light weight and green, decentralised, and of course, it is also for anyone to invest in. Nxt, at its core, cuts out the intermediaries, opens up a global marketplace, where any private person in the world can not only send money instantly over borders for low fees, but also sell goods globally, issue assets globally, share stories securely, timestamp and secure any document or file, fund businesses, pay shareholders automatically, create fully decentralised autonomous companies, set up secure polls, even issue secure customised digital currencies, all backed by the strong Nxt Network.

We have never had such a great opportunity to take control of our money, privacy and data, or to experiment with creating alternative systems before, almost for no cost.

Bringing Nxt to the world

So how do we spread the good news and bring understanding of this technology to the waiting world? The possible approaches are

14 https://nxter.org/developers

many.

Take this book for instance, which has been written for free and for NXTP's. It's published in partnership with Plaisir d'Histoire, it's promoted and marketed by Nxter.org's contributors and partners. Direct contributors to the book get a third of the net profit, Plaisir d'Histoire gets another third, and Nxter.org gets a third, which is passed through the NXTP asset as rewards to its holders. All this made easy by the Asset Exchange, and a great community.

Our hope is that the book will capture people's imagination. If you find it relevant, please recommend it to your peers, your school, your local library, or your local politicians, it all helps. Or contact us, let us know your thoughts, discuss them with other readers, find like-minded people to work with.

Still, while people reading about Nxt is good, we'd like people to actually use it. Besides offering tutorials, information about assets, coins and working 3rd party software on Nxter.org, we have recently started supporting a "NxtBridge"-project which aims to make life better for small entrepreneurs with no knowledge of coding decentralised apps:

> "NxtBridge is a base plugin for the Wordpress CMS[15], which can turn a Wordpress-powered website into an entrance point to the Nxt blockchain and p2p network. With the plugin and its add-ons, bloggers, crowdfunders, merchants, asset issuers, local communities and businesses can integrate Nxt ID login, cryptocurrency wallets, payments,

15 https://wordpress.org

smart transactions and many Nxt core features into their website, simply by pasting shortcodes".

The idea should be obvious. Nxt offers, as the only functional example, a full blockchain based financial solution for users and businesses. Bring Nxt core features to them by "bridging" Nxt (and Nxt 2.0, when the time comes) to popular CMS-systems, like Wordpress, so that they, or anyone who can perform a 5-minute Wordpress installation, can make use of Nxt: With NxtBridge plugins and the use of shortcodes, anyone can set up a website with just the Nxt features, which are relevant to him and his project. Be it for tipping authors or commenters of a blog. Be it an online shop. Be it a crowdfunding campaign, a business site, or a hub to several shops, assets or fundraising campaigns. Whatever the admin's project, it will benefit from Nxt's smart transactions, security and low fees (as opposed to the current centralised 3rd party payment services).

The user who registers can access his account balance, trading history, assets, coins, files, etc, and do it from any site which has the base NxtBridge plugin enabled, any Nxt online wallet, and also if the user decides to connect to his account from a locally hosted Nxt Client. The Wordpress site admin has no access to any of his data, ever, as the user's transactions are signed locally on the user's computer, so *his passphrase is never sent to the site server or to any Nxt node*, and all transaction details and user uploads are stored on the decentralised Nxt blockchain, which cannot be locked down.

The NxtBridge project is, at the time of writing, in development, the base plugin can be downloaded for test purposes from https://nxter.org/nxtbridge. We hope that also other Wordpress- and Nxt Service-developers will see the potential and help create additional use cases.

Have Nxter.org become self sufficient then? Well, yes - and no. A core team runs the site, pays the bills and (almost) monthly dividends. It makes general decisions, quality checks, reports, coordinate global campaigns, and filters out the scammers, who wants to get featured. We take pride in maintaining a trustful service, and when questionable new entrepreneurs, asset issuers or businesses want to pay to get advertised or have sponsored articles published, we research them - scammers will never be approved, but exposed. This we do.

But we can't pay a salary to anyone yet, and we can't hire paid workers or run paid external promotional campaigns. We are a global team, connected, committed, in it for the long term, we have quality discussions, and we may even LOL and ROFL, while working seriously on building beneficial partnerships and moving things forward. We are building a business, and we hold our Nxterpoints.

If you want to support Nxter.org, the project or the movement, a donation is appreciated and helpful[16]. If you want to get NXTP's by blogging about a relevant topic, translate, run a section or even become the editor of a new sub-site, get promoted or showcase

---

16 Donate NXT to NXT-DG6A-4BEC-4G3W-D3VCC, send dividend paying Nxt assets to NXT-EAVH-SLEV-KSEE-EE2KP or BTC to 38wAT8bCXFStHXSGyKd2EVBngRzRveR8aM. Thanks! You can earmark a donation to a project or person. Contact us @ https://nxter.org/contact

your Nxt product, or make a cooperation arrangement - contact us. If not - just enjoy our work. Stay in the loop, and educate yourself about Nxt[17]. Then take action. We'll see what we can do to help you.

17 https://nxter.org/newsletters

Nxt
Foundation
how to market a decentralised
open source organisation

 NXT Cryptocurrency

NXT FOUNDATION HOW TO MARKET A DECENTRALISED OPEN SOURCE ORGANISATION

Written by: Dave 'EvilDave' Pearce

Origins of the Nxt Foundation

One of the great strengths of Nxt, and of the wider Nxt community is that it has always been intended, from the initial Nxt concept onwards, that Nxt would be a strongly decentralised community.

A very useful guide to the basic principles of decentralised organisation can be found in 'The Starfish and the Spider' by Ori Brafman[1].

A decentralised organisation may be fine for certain applications (such as an activist movement) but for a software system that needs to interface with the wider business community, how can decentralisation work effectively ?

This issue cropped up very early on in Nxt development, giving rise to further questions:

---

1 https://en.wikipedia.org/wiki/The_Starfish_and_the_Spider

- Nxt is a brilliant system to build business applications on, but how does a business get in touch with a decentralised movement like the Nxt Community?
- How does a business enter into a legal agreement with Nxt, or receive support?
- How can Nxt be promoted to businesses, or carry out PR?

The answers to all of the above led to the setup of the Nxt Foundation[2], which (if we go back to the 'Starfish' analogy) can be seen as a specialised organ for Nxt, like an extra leg for the starfish.

The Foundation was created to act as a sub-section of the Nxt ecosystem that is responsible for linking the decentralised, open-source community of Nxt with the very much centralised mainstream business and finance world. In effect acting as a gateway between the decentralised crypto world and the centralised mainstream worlds of business, finance and governance.

The Foundation was initially (informally) set up in mid 2014, by a group of veterans of the fledgling Nxt community. The main personnel involved were: Tai 'Tai Zen' Duong, David 'EvilDave' Pearce , Bas 'Damelon' Wisselink, Dirk 'LocoMB' Reuter and Ian 'Chanc3r' Ravenscroft. As befits a decentralised organisation, the initial founding members represented a wide range of viewpoints and possessed a very wide range of skills.

This group first met in real life as representatives for Nxt at the groundbreaking BitCoin2014 conference, held in Amsterdam, and

2 http://www.nxtfoundation.io

worked so well together that they decided to carry on under the then informal banner of the Nxt Foundation.

Initially simply a loose group intended as a contact point for businesses, the Nxt Foundation proved themselves to be very useful to Nxt, and began to evolve into a fully fledged business unit with wider ranging responsibilities.

The Foundation was registered and incorporated at the start of 2015 as a non-profit business in the Netherlands, under the title of 'Stichting Nxt/Nxt Foundation' with the goal of supporting Nxt development and expansion.

Since then, the Nxt Foundation has continued to function as a contact point for businesses who wish to work with Nxt , and has also taken on other responsibilities: the purchase and maintenance of essential software, such as SSL and code signing certificates, developer licenses and hosting for Nxt-core related sites. Most recently, the Foundation identified some areas that needed to be improved within Nxt, and set up the Tennessee Project to address those areas.

Entering Tennessee

Towards mid-2015, it became increasingly obvious that Nxt needed to change to meet the demands of a rapidly changing crypto-currency market: many mainstream players were entering the market, bringing with them from the mainstream business/finance world a more professional approach to project management and a much more aggressive approach to PR and marketing.

A decentralised (and somewhat under-funded) project that relied on volunteer work, like Nxt, could not compete on an equal footing with the professional marketing and PR employed by this new wave of crypto projects.

Individual projects based on Nxt, usually with a defined project leader or a small group of leaders, could easily choose for themselves whether or not to follow this trend, or how to respond to the changes in the market, but for the Nxt core (and the wider Nxt community) a solution had to be found to address this situation.

Thus the Tennessee project was proposed: the Nxt Foundation analysed and explained the current market situation to the community, and asked them to donate to a Foundation administered fund set up purely to professionalise and improve two basic elements of the Nxt core project: Marketing/PR and the user experience. The estimated budget to run Tennessee for a year (on the basis of two part-time employees) was approximately $70,000 or 10 million NXT. This sum was raised via crowdfunding (using the Nxt Monetary System) inside 2 weeks, and Tennessee went live at the start of November 2015.

So, coming back to the original question: how does a decentralised community promote itself to the outside world ?

Nxt has shown, with the creation of the Nxt Foundation and subsequently the Tennessee project, that organically created specialised systems can be set up to fulfil this specific function, without sacrificing any of the openness and decentralisation that give the Nxt community a great degree of both flexibility and strength.

Achievements

Written by EvilDave on September 5th, 2016

The TNSSE project is now a year further on since the above piece was written, and approaching the end of the funding period. The Nxt Foundation has, over the last year, achieved many of the goals outlined in the original TNSSE proposal[3], and a lot more besides:

Nxt's web presence has been completely overhauled, with a new www.nxt.org site, and a new site for the Foundation itself: www.nxtfoundation.io.

Marketing has been massively improved, with a 3 man team having been recruited to professionalise Nxt's entire marketing strategy: John McLeod, Mitchell Lureiro and Travin Keith have taken Nxt marketing to a much higher level, and will continue to do so for Nxt and for the Nxt 2.0 project[4].

The Foundation has, as a result of the TNSSE funding, been able to

---

3 https://nxtforum.org/general-discussion/(marketing-business-and-development)-the-tennessee-project-fundraiser
4 https://www.ardorplatform.org

sponsor the monthly 'Bitcoin Wednesday'[5] meetups in Amsterdam, giving Nxt a very effective platform for presentations and networking.

As part of the Nxt Foundation's strategy to build bridges between communities, we joined the Linux Foundation as a means of reaching out to the wider Open Source community. This has led to a small role within the Hyperledger blockchain project, rubbing shoulders with the likes of JP Morgan and Wells Fargo.

Nxt Foundation has an office! The TNSSE funding allowed the Foundation to rent an office in the center of Amsterdam[6], giving us a very representative and professional venue for our activities.

Less visibly, the Foundation has put a lot of effort into networking and business development, and we are in active talks with several potential partners for blockchain projects from both business and government. As part of our outreach program, we are looking at setting up elements of academic programs in partnership with a couple of Dutch educational institutions, helping to encourage new talent to come on board with blockchain and Nxt.

The Foundation itself has been expanded, with new members and partners coming on board to bring their unique skills and experience to Nxt: http://www.nxtfoundation.io/
Lastly: Nxt now has, uniquely among major cryptocurrencies/blockchain platforms, a professional support desk: nxt.org/helpdesk/.

---

5 http://www.bitcoinwednesday.com
6 https://www.nxtforum.org/general-discussion/(tnnse)-tennessee-updates/msg210490/#msg210490

Set up by TestDruif (whose day job is that of support specialist), and manned by volunteers from the Nxt community, the helpdesk has handled hundreds of support requests in a very effective fashion.

NXT
the original spirit

 NXT Cryptocurrency

THE ORIGINAL SPIRIT

Written by: Bas 'Damelon' Wisselink

From 28th September 2013 to 24th November 2013, a developer calling himself "BCNext" was seen posting on the bitcointalk forums about his new project which would subsequently become Nxt. From the start, he made it clear that this project would not be carried by him but that instead, whilst it would embody the original spirit of the Bitcoin project, it should be developed in a decentralised, leaderless way.

After some 8 weeks of posting about the project, he removed his known persona from the discussion by ceasing to speak via his "BCNext" account. Whether or not he is still keeping an eye on the project or otherwise somehow contributing to it under a different name is unknown, but from that moment on the Nxt project lost its figurehead.

Decentralisation

Decentralisation is a hard topic to pin down. It is a historical fact that humans tend to congregate in groups that form clusters and these clusters are as a rule led by a leader or leaders. This is not only a cultural habit, it is a behaviour that we see all around the animal kingdom, and especially in groups of primates. The behaviour can be very beneficial.

Having a smaller group to make decisions for the larger group allows for more efficient decision making and works well in crises. On the other hand, it also means you draw on a smaller pool of knowledge and can lead to marginalisation of individuals and an unhealthy concentration of power. One of the most perilous periods in any monarchy tended to be times of succession, which often led to bloodshed and civil war, before a clear winner emerged and set him or herself up as the sole leader.

For the purposes of this chapter, when I speak about decentralisation I mean a movement that aims to remove the 'leader' or 'decision-maker' as a bottleneck or Single Point of Failure. Confusion regarding the meaning and use of the term 'decentralisation' has been a recurring theme in the history of Nxt and crypto-communities in general. Hence the need for clarity.

Confusion

I also want to distinguish between decentralisation of the Network on the one hand, and decentralisation of the Community on the other.

The decentralisation of the Network solves a very specific problem and is expressed in code. The decentralisation of the Community is an ideological stance that is expressed in explicit and implicit rules and behaviours. It is easy to confuse the two, as indeed has frequently happened.

The Nxt community's development can be seen as an exploration of management, grassroots development, open source initiatives, and free software.

Nxt community and development

Over the course of the last two years, Nxt has been developed by a group of independent developers working together in a loose partnership. The mainstay of this group has been the developer going by the nickname of "Jean-Luc" in honor of Jean Luc Picard of the USS Enterprise. From the start, having refactored the code written by BCNext, Jean-Luc has been hard at work continuing to develop it.

While developers are vital to Nxt, they do not 'lead' the project. The Nxt project is not led in any conventional sense, but rather functions by virtue of individuals starting initiatives which are either successful or fail. This process is not nearly as hit and miss as you might think. Instead, it favours innovation and creates an ever-open field where anyone can try and only the people with the requisite business and organisation skills will flourish.

This explains why people looking in on the Nxt community from the outside often get the impression of a disjointed, disorganised group of people talking at cross purposes. Some may find this off-putting, especially those who take the view that progress can only be made in a linear way where the dots are clearly marked out in advance and always joined by straight lines.

However, a more accurate way of looking at a project like Nxt, and for instance also Linux, is that people independently of each other put down their dots and then afterwards look round to see if it's possible to connect them to other dots which have been put down by others. This means that the picture of what is possible is emerging and growing, instead of being predefined and limited.

The movement of decentralised development is lateral and oblique rather than linear.

Leadership and decentralisation

This does not mean that 'decentralisation' must necessarily involve the abandoning of leadership. Businesses still need to be founded in common sense. Spending resources, be it money or time, without any plan at all is always of course a bad idea. Decentralisation may mean questioning standard practices, but it does not mean it cannot arrive at answers that have been shown to work.

Projects are still put forward by either small groups or individuals with an idea. Because they hold the blueprint in their minds, they typically assume leadership roles within their projects. Even when they decide to share responsibility regarding their projects once bootstrapped, they generally still have significant influence over their development.

The Nxt project itself, as a leaderless project, still has no central leadership. From the start, several individuals have taken up responsibility for the general welfare of the community, but no one person, acting on their own, is able to make definitive decisions.

At the time of writing, decisions are in effect being made by a system of market and development pressures. The core developers propose or code Nxt to behave in certain ways. In response users and 3rd party developers can and do, often vigorously, voice their assent or displeasure with these changes through various channels including the Nxt Forums, Slack, or by publishing articles. Normally, these changes are made via patches, or it is explained why these will not be made or must be postponed.

If such decisions are not accepted, the process usually becomes heated. This is where decentralised decision making can be confusing to people who are used to centralised processes. Decentralised processes are by their nature vocal and not everyone involved is necessarily skilled at expressing themselves. This part of the process can therefore be long and arduous, but the flipside of it is that a lot of knowledge and view-points are exchanged, which in turn provide nourishment for future developments. Due to the skill and merit-based nature of decentralised processes, this is usually the time where individuals with negotiating skills come into their own.

A decentralised organisation often looks like pure chaos when looked at from the outside. Rule-like conformity and sticking to a coherent plan are often seen to be ignored or even absent.

Still, it would be a profound mistake to think that decentralisation is equal to chaos, because while there may not be a concrete blue-print to get from A to B, the fact that decentralised organisations do get the work done, and often quicker than centrally led ones, is proof that there must be some kind of process going on.

Decentralised organisations more often form around ideas than around fully formulated end goals. This allows for quick re-evaluation of objectives and changing plans on the move. Where a fully planned campaign might break down due to changing circumstances, a decentralised organisation takes these in its stride and adjusts.

Again, this looks like chaos to people who are not accustomed to it. At no point is there a fixed plan to get from A to B. The challenge in a decentralised organisation is to keep ones eyes firmly on B, while the route taken is far less important. Offshoots of the organisation will develop along the way, when people stumble on C and D and decide these are more interesting to them than the original goal. But the main drive of the organisation will still be to get to B.

Nxt Foundation

An interesting property of a decentralised organisation is that the 'head' of an organisation is just as loosely attached to the main body as all the other parts. An interesting analogy that has been made is between spiders and starfish when comparing centrally led organisations and decentralised ones.

When you cut off the head of a spider, the organism dies. However, in a starfish, there is no head. Instead, if you cut off one of its limbs, both the original organism and the limb will survive.

You can also see this happening in Nxt. Its community is made up of several branches that could be cut off without affecting the body as a whole. They could also split off and venture forth without the main body.

The Nxt Foundation is an example of how a leaderless project can still have an outward facing section that acts as a leader, while not having the same empowerments that traditional leaders have.

The Nxt Foundation was started when a few members of the community saw that there was a need for an organisation that was recognised by the outside world as Nxt's representative. These members, who all have a background in business, saw that mainstream businesses were uncomfortable engaging with a decentralised organisation on its own terms. Their answer: set up a separate registered organisation and act like a centralised business to the outside world, while internally working in a decentralised manner.

The Nxt Foundation took the Linux Foundation as its inspiration. Its stated goal is not management, but facilitation. Like water flows more easily through even channels, the Foundation aims to create those channels for use by both the community and the business world. Its main focus of operation is education about the new platform, both for the outside world and the community itself.

To the outside world, the Foundation fulfils the role of being a recognisable structure with which to interact. The larger part of the Nxt community has accepted the need for the Foundation and so, by consensus, it is able to fulfil its self-appointed role. The nature of the decentralised organisation means that as long as the community supports it, it can function. When this support ceases, it will either need to adapt, or die off.

Nxt, past and future

When I was asked to write this chapter, I initially thought of taking a historical approach. However I soon decided this would not do proper justice to what I consider to be the greatest strength of the Nxt Project.

When I first entered the world of cryptocurrencies, there were many projects to choose from. Nxt stood out for me, because as a project it embodied the things that I have always valued in both my personal and professional life: innovation, daring, fun, entrepreneurship and above all a freedom of spirit.

The fact that Nxt has been able to stay true to the original spirit of decentralisation even when developing parts of its organisation that need to interact with businesses is a testament to the strength of this model.

During the past year, multiple projects have been started that operate in the same environment, but are centrally led. These, so far, have failed to attract the attention that one would have expected from the big marketing resources that have been spent on them.

Nxt meanwhile has stayed under the radar, but has nevertheless managed an impressive speed of development at a fraction of the costs. The community is vibrant and positive, while aware of the many possible pitfalls. There is a willingness to question anything and everyone up to and including the members of the core developers' team. In a centrally led organisation this would be seen as a weakness, in Nxt it is a strength.

Whilst interacting on the forums everyone working on Nxt will, at some time or another, feel challenged to think about the core values they want to see embodied in their system of choice.

Just a bland synchronic account would not do the project justice. As a decentralised project that is open to people, we can be sure that we will face the same problems over and over again. Developers will never be able to sit on their laurels and merely create what they like. Even if the senior members of the community accept this, there is bound to be someone without their knowledge of past events that will ask questions and open up the debate once again. And this is good!

A decentralised organisation does not grow towards a perfect configuration: it grows and lives and continues to be emergent. Once it stagnates and solidifies, it dies. With this in the back of my mind, I wish Nxt many years of productive conflict and unexpected turns.

As long as it can surprise us, it certainly can surprise the world.

NXT

aliases

NXT Cryptocurrency

ALIASES

Written by: apenzl, Cassius

The Alias feature was released with block 22,000, on 22nd of December 2013.

As soon as Aliasing was enabled, aliases with commercial potential were grabbed by Nxters who hoped that they might one day be able to sell them on at a vast profit – just like domain squatting on the web. Brands and big corporation names were bought for the bargain sum of 1 NXT – along with a lot of sex-related aliases, of many and highly diverse permutations. Later, a bot was even used to hoover up every word of up to four letters that hadn't already been registered.

Aliasing allows one piece of text to be substituted for another, so that keywords or key phrases can be used to represent other things – names, telephone numbers, physical addresses, web sites, account numbers, email addresses, product SKU codes... almost anything you can think of.

The most obvious use for Aliases is simply to make it easier to send NXT. By registering an alias and pointing it to a NXT account address you no longer have to specify that address when sending coins or messages to it from the Nxt Client; instead just send the coins and messages to the alias and they will be received by the connected NXT account.

Chrome and Firefox browser plugins that use the Alias system to replace domain names have been developed – making it possible, for example, by entering nxt:search into your browser, to go to Google.com, or by entering nxt:mysite to surf to https://mysite.xyz. The alias could be re-directed to a backup clone of that site, if mysite.xyz for any reason was taken down. Remember: You must trust an alias owner not to link to a malicious website!

Nxt lead developer Jean-Luc publishes SHA-256 for the latest NRS software using alias: 'NRSversion', this alias is then used by the client wallet to determine if the current client version is up to date[1]. Another example which is worth mentioning is the use of the Alias feature for uploading profile page data to NxtMemo, an early (not up-to-date) decentralised micro-messaging platform[2].

The ability to store aliases with arbitrary data has also been leveraged to store domain name/aliases to IP address mappings on the mesh. With a DNS bridge like NxtHypeDns[3] you can use the Nxt system and its aliases to resolve domain names into Hyperboria[4] meshnet compatible ipv6 address. Sites on Hyperboria meshnet are mostly accessed by typing their ipv6 addresses, for example: http://[1234:4564:3452:4675:3453:2344]. But with the Nxt DNS bridge, users can simply use Nxt Aliases to map to the ipv6 address, and there is no longer a need for them to type and remember the long numeric addresses.

---

1 https://www.mynxt.info/alias/15746067221582034079
2 https://nxtforum.org/nxtmemo/nxtmemo-twitter-clone-based-on-nxt-messaging-system/msg97863
3 https://github.com/slothbag/NxtHypeDns
4 Hyperboria is an encrypted Mesh Network designed for privacy and resiliency to censorship. Website: https://hyperboria.net

An alias currently costs 2 NXT to register. Aliases can be transfer-red, and offered for sale.

On https://www.mynxt.info/aliases you can search for an alias and see whether it is for sale.

NXT

arbitrary messages

NXT Cryptocurrency

ARBITRARY MESSAGES

Written by: apenzl, Cassius

The Arbitrary Message (AM) feature was released with block 40,000, on 11th of January, 2014.

The feature enables Nxt users to send small amounts of either open or encrypted data to the blockchain. Arbitrary Messages commonly take the form of SMS-length communications between users. This was the first application and is still one of the most popular uses for AMs, but the term 'message' is a loose one: as well as being used to send encrypted messages to each other, at the most basic level creating a decentralised private chat system, AMs can be used to send and store any form of data on the blockchain. A simple concept in theory, but the applications for this feature are extensive.

There are, of course, many valid use cases for unencrypted messages also. Announcements, micro-blogging, or the famous example of AMs sent to the hacker who stole 51 million NXT from the BTer exchange's hot wallet on August 15, 2014[1,2]; it was via unencrypted AMs that negotiations were started with the hacker.

Advanced applications can use AMs to store structured data, such as JSON objects. These can be used to trigger or facilitate 3rd party

---

1 https://nxtforum.org/news-and-announcements/forgers-have-been-faced-with-a-choice/msg81782

2 https://cointelegraph.com/news/cointelegraph-interviews-cobaltskky-the-butt-that-saved-bter

services built on top of Nxt. For example, deposit and withdrawal requests for SuperNET's early MultiGateWay (MGW) service[3] are broadcast as AMs[4] when a user transfers Bitcoins and other supported cryptocurrencies to the distributed exchange, which allows for direct peer-to-peer trading.

NXT FreeMarket[5], a decentralised marketplace built on top of Nxt, uses AMs to store shop data, descriptions and pictures of goods for sale, and Helix[6], which aims to become a disruptive standalone cross-platform financial analytics and visualisation client, uses AMs as data containers to store whole apps. Helix loads, concatenates, decompresses and decrypts these AMs directly from the blockchain, where they are stored, into memory. A fast, clean and secure solution which has a number of important real-world advantages:

1.   It makes apps independent and robust against attacks.
2.   It provides nearly unrestricted access from anywhere due to the decentralised storage.
3.   It provides on-the-fly autorepair and update capabilities[7].

Dapp storage, however, was not intended for NXT 1.0, support for it can be added with Nxt 2.0.

Another advanced feature of encrypted messages is the shared key which allows encrypted messages between two accounts to be shared with a 3rd party account or announced publicly. This feature

---

3 http://multigateway.org
4 Documentation: http://multigateway.org/downloads/Multigateway_docs.pdf
5 http://www.nxtfreemarket.com
6 http://finhive.com/fh_helix.html
7 Source: https://nxtforum.org/nxt-projects/helix-dapps-test-cp-repos

can be used for example in the use case of medical records when Dr. Alice shares encrypted diagnosis with patient Bob who can later share this encrypted information with Dr. Charley without making it public.

Data Cloud

The Nxt Data Cloud feature can be seen as an extension of unencrypted AMs, with searchable metadata fields[8] added. It can be used for decentralised and trustless distribution of small pieces of data, one obvious use case being the (censorship-free) distribution of documents, signed and timestamped so that they can't be tampered with. It is not a hosting platform for sharing or publishing larger files like mp3, images or videos (unless what you share is actually a magnet link), as the file size is limited to 42 kilobytes[9].

Storage time

Both AMs and the cloud data work with prunable data[10]; meaning that the uploaded files (by default) are discarded from the blockchain in regular nodes after 90 days (this has been implemented to prevent blockchain bloat), after which only the hash of the data remains in the blockchain. The data items are still available from

---

8 Tagged data: https://nxtwiki.org/wiki/The_Nxt_API#Tagged_Data_Operations
9 This is due to change with the release of Nxt 2.0 childchains, https://nxter.org/ardor
10 Nxt Blockchain pruning: https://nxtwiki.org/wiki/The_Nxt_API#Prunable_Data

archival nodes[11] and can be verified against the blockchain even after their expiration. Another option is extending the lifetime of the data item for a fee, so that it is stored longer or indefinitely in the blockchain.

---

11 Archival nodes are nodes that keep all the previously pruned data in their data base. Each node has an algorithm to locate other archival nodes. As long as just one archival node contains your data, the other nodes will find it.

NXT

the asset exchange

NXT Cryptocurrency

THE ASSET EXCHANGE

Written by: apenzl, Cassius, Zahlen

"AE is changing the world".

~ theironman

"Holy shit, I forged a block with 5010 NXT in fees. That's more than what forging machine is worth. If you have NXT and don't forge – you really should start"...

~ iruu

The Nxt Asset Exchange[1] was released at block height 135000, on May 12th, 2014.

NXT coins can be designated to represent other crypto coins, fiat, stocks/bonds, property, commodities, precious metals, or even ideas. Most cryptocurrencies operate as merely currencies, but since the blockchain provides a trustworthy and permanent ledger of all transactions, it can be used to record far more diverse information than purely currency transactions. The Asset Exchange (AE) is Nxt's built-in decentralised trading engine.

The AE is based on the 'coloured coins' concept[2], the blockchain's ability to recognise and therefore trace the origin of transactions involving a coin or a set of coins which have been designated to represent something else – opening up wide-ranging possibilities.

---

1 https://nxtwiki.org/wiki/Asset_Exchange
2 https://github.com/Colored-Coins/Colored-Coins-Protocol-Specification/wiki/
Introduction

These crypto-assets can gain significant market cap, and many Nxt assets are listed on sites like CoinMarketCap.com. It currently costs only 1000 NXT to issue an asset, and 1 NXT in transaction fee to buy or sell them. As well as being traded on the Nxt AE against NXT, some of these assets can also be traded against Bitcoin on centralised exchanges.

Over 700 assets have been issued to date, a few are described elsewhere in this book. Some were issued as experiments (HUGS; Hugs are not for getting rich. It's for spreading, baby! This asset is sold at the lowest price possible and it doesn't pay dividends), others represent real shares in newly started or existing companies. Some issuers have raised small amounts, others have raised millions. Some assets are sold in IPO's, others in Dutch Auctions, some have turned out to be issued by scammers, some have given their investors more than a decent ROI.

New asset announcements are often made on nxtforum.org/asset-board. A list of all issued assets and their live and past performance on the AE can be found on mynxt.info. Also, a list of assets, which are selected and recommended by AE traders, can be found on nxter.org/assethub, with interviews of the issuers and updates being added regularly.

Caveat emptor!

The AE is decentralised and currently completely unregulated. The substantial benefits this offers – cost savings, lack of intervention, freedom, and so on – also come at a price. There is no hand-holding or policing - only the knowledge gained from trial and error by the Nxt Community. If a long-standing member of the community with a proven track-record issues an asset, there is more reason for confidence than if a newcomer does – no matter how impressive their sales pitch. Scam assets are easy to create and promote, and if you make a mistake then there is very little recourse as transactions are irreversible. The responsibility to check out an asset, its issuer and business plan before you buy into it is - of course - ultimately yours!

After the launch of Nxt 2.0, KYC & regulated child chains can be issued[3].

Other relevant features

Several features have been added to the core since the release of the AE, which expands the use of the it, including:

- a dividend payment feature for asset issuers which allows them to distribute NXT to their asset holders according to their pro-

---

3 "[With Nxt 2.0] a child chain can be limited to support only a subset of the globally available transaction types, thus excluding features that are not needed by the specific child chain creator business, are undesirable, or have legal restrictions in their jurisdiction", lead developer Jean-Luc writes. Also, "child chains can enforce further rules on transactions denominated in their token, such as permissioning, limiting which accounts are authorized to issue specific transaction types, in order to e.g. comply with KYC rules for a child chain pegged to a fiat currency, or assets marketed to a jurisdiction imposing additional restrictions on who can trade them". Source: https://nxtforum.org/core-development-announcements/nxt-2-0-overview/msg217738

portional asset shares for only a 1 NXT fee[4].

- a voting-feature - whereby, for example, asset holders can be invited to vote on important issues regarding the asset they hold (by weight of stake or with one vote each).

- smart transactions - transactions can be programmed to be executed only if a specified precondition is met. For example, that the transaction is signed by two or more pre-defined parties, (e.g. company executives or shareholders) or that the majority of shareholders vote in favour of a transaction for it to be (automatically) executed. Moreover, transactions can be set to be executed at a pre-defined date and time. The smart (multi phased) transactions make it possible to easily set up a DAO[5] on the Nxt Blockchain.

- Singleton assets can be issued to represent a 'one of a kind' asset such as a specific car, apartment or a unique jewelry piece so that applications can be implemented to unlock this specific asset based on asset ownership or track the asset lawful owner.

Assets issued with Nxt 2.0 will become tradeable across all Ardor[6] child chains, and will - with child chains pegged to fiat, and other child chains pegged to, for example, crypto coins like Bitcoin - become tradeable on a much bigger market, in effect, creating a fully decentralised, multi currency, fast, low fee, globally scalable market for any kind of asset.

---

4 With a locally running script like the free Nxt Plugin 'Dividend payout' you can distribute asset dividends also (be it fiat- or cryptocoin-pegged assets, bonus points, company shares, or something else), but it will cost you a 1 NXT fee per transaction, i.e. 1 NXT x the number of your asset holders.
5 https://en.wikipedia.org/wiki/Decentralized_autonomous_organization
6 Ardor is the name of Nxt 2.0, read more in the chapter: 'Nxt 2.0; ARDOR'.

NXT

crowdfunding

 NXT Cryptocurrency

NXT CROWDFUNDING

Written by: RubénBC[1]

In the last few years crowdfunding has enjoyed a remarkable rise. Nxt is the perfect platform for doing fundraising and following it up by actually running the business.

Crowdfunding platforms bring together people who have a small amount of money to invest and people who have a project that needs funding. However, while the centrally controlled crowdfunding platforms are promoted as being inexpensive and easy to use, in practice they are not:

The entrepreneur and the small investors have to register with those centrally controlled platforms. The profile of the entrepreneur and the nature of the project itself has to be approved by the platform, and it has to meet all the other terms of service (these platforms have their own specific conditions for any entrepreneur), for example: exclusivity (if listed on the platform your project cannot be listed elsewhere), you must work with banks from a specific country or even a specific bank etc.

Adding to that, the payments are usually carried out through a third party payment platform. The payment platform (as distinct from the crowdfunding platform) is in charge of managing all the money which people invest and, if the target amount isn't reached, paying the investors back. During this time, it is the payment

---

1 Rubén is writer and editor for NXTER.ORG/es (Spanish)

platform which holds the money, not the investors nor the fund-raiser, and at the end of the crowdfunding period, if the monetary objectives are fulfilled, the payment platform has to be trusted to release the money to the entrepreneur, excluding the fees that the crowdfunding platform charges. For example, at the time of writing, Kickstarter, which is probably the best known crowdfunding platform, charges 5% of the total amount collected, plus 3% and €2 from every donation made! [2]

The Nxt Monetary System

Nxt's alternative to conventional and centralized crowdfunding websites is the platform's Monetary System (MS)[3], that was launched on January 10th, 2015. This allows users to create their own decentralized currencies, guaranteed by Nxt's blockchain. This system, in addition to the Asset Exchange, makes Nxt the most comprehensive and decentralised financial crowdfunding tool available, enabling its users to liberate themselves from centralised fiat based control, and from paying high fees to the various middlemen riding this system.

Coins issued in the Nxt Monetary System are fully customizable, thereby allowing them to be used for a wide variety of use cases; for example, if you want to start a crowdfunding campaign using the Nxt platform, select the parameters "reservable" and "exchangeable" for the campaign's currency. This configuration allows

---

2 https://www.kickstarter.com/help/fees
3 https://nxtwiki.org/wiki/Monetary_System. To read more about MS, see the chapter: 'Monetary System'

people willing to take part in the campaign to reserve a portion of this new 'coin' in exchange for some NXT, and their deposit will be reflected in the blockchain. If the funding target isn't met, the amount of NXT deposited will automatically be sent back to the contributors once the crowdfunding period is over.

On the other hand, if the financing objectives are met, the NXT deposited is immediately released to the issuer of the campaign and the 'coins' are automatically distributed among the contributors. From that moment on, the issuer can't claim the coins back.

He can send messages to the 'coin' holders, for example text updates or video-links. He can ask them to vote (for example to get reviews of his early product). He can send them dividends (could be tokens which give access to a game, coins to spend in the game, or later, even a percentage of his profit). Or he could offer to buy back the 'coins' in the exchange at market price. Any of these actions would be recorded in and secured by the blockchain, no middlemen involved.

A nice example of crowdfunding using the Nxt Monetary System is the Tennessee Project:

"The project will require 10 million NXT in order to keep the foundation working for 12 months. The Monetary System will be used to collect the money. The foundation leader, EvilDave, has issued the currency TNSSE from the account NXT- P439-YVBD-VUEQ-A3S2T. The crowdfunding will be on until the 26th of October, 2015. If we reach 10

million NXT, all the money will be transferred to the Tennessee account. If that amount isn't reached, all the money will be sent back to the donors automatically"[4].

The total fees paid to use the Nxt Monetary System for the Tennessee crowdfunding campaign was only 40 NXT! (approximately 0.28€)

Crowdfunding on the Asset Exchange

As well as using the Monetary System to fund your project, you can also use the Asset Exchange (AE). Since May 12th, 2014, the AE has been a Nxt core feature. Anyone can issue assets on this totally decentralised and uncontrolled exchange and trade them. You can monitor your Nxt asset purchases either via your client or via a number of independent websites[5].

The key feature of the Nxt AE for businesspeople is that they can fund their business via asset issuance, getting money from anyone (not just angels/VCs, as with KickStarter), and they can do so from day one and for a low fee.

By clicking on the "Issue Asset" tab in the Nxt Client you can quickly create an asset related to your project/company that others can

4 Tennessee Project's holding account: https://www.mynxt.info/account/10124938546868029479. Salary account: https://www.mynxt.info/alias/2944910803085887398
Fundraising thread: https://nxtforum.org/general-discussion/%28marketing-business-and-development%29-the-tennessee-project-fundraiser
5 Blockchain explorers like https://nxtportal.org and https://mynxt.info/block-explorer

buy, in order to support your project/company and be rewarded for their support. If you have a product or service either ready to start marketing or already being marketed, the Asset Exchange is the tool to use.

Via the Asset Exchange, you can:

- Obtain funding for your product or service.
- Sell your product or service.
- IPO @ a fixed price, or hold a Dutch auction[6].
- Interact with your asset-holders, including paying them dividends/revenue share/bonuses using NXT coins or other assets (that could include assets tied to BTC, EUR or another fiat currency).

Your assets will be instantly tradeable on the Asset Exchange.

To Issue an asset on the Nxt AE and take advantage of all the benefits it provides, you only have to pay a fee of 1000 NXT (approximately 6.5€ at the current exchange rate).

It's perfect! What is left to be solved?

These options are optimal for Nxters - but, and there is always a 'but'... If your potential funders do not own NXT or BTC, they will currently have to buy NXT, to reap all the benefits and invest in

---

6 https://en.wikipedia.org/wiki/Dutch_auction
Example: https://nxtforum.org/news-and-announcements/(ann)-jinn

your project. It doesn't take much effort to get NXT[7], but until cryptocurrencies have been more widely adopted, this is still an extra step between you and your potential funders, a test of their laziness against their goodwill or business sense.

What if the value of NXT tokens suddenly crumbles to dust? It should cause a revaluation of your asset, which will probably rise in terms of NXT, as the asset is backed by something which has not lost any value. But what does it mean to you? Well, you crowdfunded in NXT. Simply put: You would still have lost part of the money, which you raised for your project.

The Nxt core does not yet offer a built-in solution to these scenarios. One solution could be to move the NXT raised into a (more) stable asset like NxtUSD, which is pegged to the US dollar, after you have reached your crowdfunding goal. The asset pays 0.06% daily interest on your NxtUSD holdings in your NXT account. Maybe you need to pay your rent or pay employees in fiat money, so at times you would cash some of the raised funds out to your bank account. Moving NxtUSD to any VISA/Mastercard costs a fee of around 3%.

That said, others, like us crypto geeks, would never choose to exchange NXT to fiat. Several merchants and services take payments in BTC. To cash out large amounts of NXT to BTC (without crashing the NXT market), you could buy SuperBTC[8] for NXT on the AE or

---

7 Anyone can exchange fiat or Bitcoins to NXT, see a list of exchanges here: https://nxter.org/exchanges
8 SuperBTC is an asset on the AE, which represents 1 BTC 1:1 and can be sent directly to BTC wallets using SuperNET's MultiGateWay (MGW) service. For more information, visit http://multigateway.org

use a service like Liquid OnDemand[9]. The exchange is made with tradebots, the fee is 2.5%.

Asset issuers can also arrange with central exchanges to list their assets and (if necessary) pass on their dividends to their holders on the exchange, though it is not advisable, as you will have to trust the people at the exchange to honor this agreement, and also because central exchanges can (and unfortunately often are) a target of hackers.

With the release of Nxt 2.0 childchains, Nxt assets will become instantly tradeable in other (maybe regulated[10]) childchain markets and currencies as well. The Nxt Monetary System's crowdfunding feature will also work universally, so that you can run crowdfunding campaigns in all sidechain currencies, like currencies pegged to for example fiat or Bitcoin.

Who dunnit?

Issuers of crowdfunding MS coins or assets on the AE must prepare themselves to be cross-examined by the Nxt Community. If you come with a sound business plan and a good reputation, this should not be a problem. But anyone with a 1000 NXT can issue an asset, and an asset token being ultimately just a promise to the as-

---

9 http://www.liquidtech.info, https://nxtforum.org/liquid/liquid-ondemand
10 https://en.wikipedia.org/wiki/Know_your_customer. [Editor's note: Nxt enables this with 'Account Properties'. Account Properties can be used for assigning arbitrary name/value metadata to user accounts so that they can be used to Whitelist accounts for a specific application or provide public data about the account owner. Another Nxt feature, the 'funding monitor' feature uses account properties in order to identify the accounts to be funded and specify the funding amounts and schedule].

set buyer by the issuer, especially in this unregulated environment, interested buyers will (and should!) do an in-depth check to see if the issuer/fundraiser can make good on their promises, before they decide whether or not to accept the risk and invest. The community will weigh the risks against potential returns before deciding if, and how much, they want to spend on a project, or invest in a business. The Nxt network cannot enforce any issuer's promises.

I recently had an opportunity of talking with the person responsible for creating and managing the Spanish Hedge Fund, BitcoinTrust SL's asset on the Nxt platform, and launching its crowdfunding campaign. BitcoinTrust SL is on Nxter.org's list of assets, which have been rated and reviewed by AE traders. To mention just a few, assets like Farla (Dutch webdesign company), LQD (Forex and crypto trading), DeBuNe (Decentralised Business Network), Jinn (the first modern ternary general purpose processor), SuperNET (Iguana tech, blockchain middleware, portfolio of cryptocurrency- and asset investments), Sigwo, and CORE, are also among the assets, which can be found @ nxter.org/assethub.

Nxt crowdfunding case study

Q: What led you to use Nxt as a crowdfunding platform for your project?

A: Actually, Nxt isn't the first funding method we've used. We previously raised money from private investors and other investors using litecoininvest.com where, for some years now, it's been possible to raise finance in the form of Bitcoin and Litecoin.

I've known about the Nxt platform since its inception and I've followed its amazing development closely. There are some alternatives like Counterparty or Mastercoin that work on Bitcoin's blockchain, but they are less usable and versatile than Nxt. So I think Bitcoin can't compete in this respect with Nxt's decentralized economical platform. I see Bitcoin as a store of value, while Nxt offers a much wider variety of possibilities.

The jump to Nxt came about because of my personal suggestion to the company owner Miquel, who allowed me to manage this fund after a small introduction about what Nxt could offer. After all, Nxt fitted perfectly with the company background: new technologies powered by blockchain.

Q: What does your company do?

A: Our main company, BitcoinTrust SL, is made up of several, wholly or partly owned, smaller companies. The main wholly owned company is called ATMs Bitcoin Exchange SLU and specialises in selling Bitcoin ATMs. The income being the fees charged to users of the ATM and the sale price of the ATM machines themselves. We produce two different sizes of ATM machine both of which are built by BTCFacil (of which we own 40%).

We also own 100% of BitPhone, a website where you can recharge the balance of your prepaid mobile phone for many carriers all around the world; 40% of Cryptobit, a company that's developing a software solution for retail shops so that they can easily accept Bitcoins and receive either Bitcoins or Euros; 15% of Bit2me, where you can buy or sell Bitcoins online using any ATM from the network Hallcash; 16,67% of HashingWorl, a website dedicated to scrypt and sha256 mining; and finally we are responsible for managing the investing related platform litecoininvest.com. We also make profit from trading surplus liquidity.

Q: Why do you need funding?

A: Funding is necessary to speed up the company growth, to build new ATMs (there are a large amount of customers showing interest in them), to invest in mining equipment, and, especially, acting as a paid counterparty for private clients buying/selling Bitcoins.

Q: How can a company earn the trust needed for people to want to invest in it?

A: That's a difficult question to answer. Like all new things it can be scary and lead to uncertainties, but the best way to gain credibility is by showing results. And our company has obtained good results for over a year. This credibility shouldn't depend on the crowdfunding system used, but on the people behind the project. Personally, I've always been very careful when investing in any project where I didn't know who was in charge.

Q: Has the Nxt platform met all your expectations?

A: For the time being, the platform has fulfilled all our needs, but I'd like to attract more people to the fund. Concerning the managing of the fund in the platform, it's been very easy. Mostly I just sell in the Asset Exchange the NXT I received from the investors in exchange for Bitcoin. Then the company puts that money to work and they pay me a weekly dividend, that I use to buy back NXT and send them to the investors as dividends. I'm considering paying dividends directly using Bitcoin, Litecoin, USD or EUR using assets like SuperBTC from the Multigateway or NxtUSD. All of that though in a decentralised way, using the Nxt Asset Exchange.

Q: Do you think that decentralised crowdfunding will be the path forward in the future?

A: Yes, I think so. But to be successful it needs more real projects with people that publicly stick up for it in order to differentiate these good projects from other projects related to cryptocurrencies and crypto platforms that are scams. Those things only give cryptocurrencies a bad name. If used properly, Nxt crowdfunding has an incredible potential and capabilities compared to conventional crowdfunding that has higher fees and other issues.

An even better way to finance your project in NXT and giving people even more sense of security could be to use the Monetary System, where the money will only be given to the company if the target amount is achieved. Otherwise, the money is automatically returned to the investors. However, in our situation we weren't seeking to achieve a concrete figure but a continuous inflow of new investors, so we chose to use the more 'traditional' Assets' system. This allows us to pay dividends easily to any holder, and they can also sell their shares any time on the Asset Exchange.

NXT

a fully decentralised marketplace

NXT Cryptocurrency

A FULLY DECENTRALISED MARKETPLACE

Written by: apenzl, Cassius

The Nxt Marketplace was released with block 210000, on 1st of August, 2014.

Although it was designed for buying and selling digital merchandise – music, ebooks, software, and so on – physical items are also listed for sale. Nxt's decentralised Marketplace enables direct peer-to-peer trading - there are absolutely no middlemen involved, no-one registers your personal information, there are no central servers which can be taken down (and therefore no single-point-of-failure), and no third-party payment processor to take a cut of the sales.

You can list goods with ease, set a price, upload a picture, change or cancel listings, communicate safely with customers through encrypted private messages on the Nxt blockchain.

Buyers are able to search for goods by issuer, item name or by tag (category). Buyers can set an order expiration date, and also leave private or public feedback after receiving a product.

Costs are limited to the transaction fees and the cost of exchanging messages (currently 1 NXT). The base fee for listing an item is 2 NXT, with an extra 2 NXT additional fee for each 32 characters (chars) of description, after the first 32 chars (name plus description, total length). The base fee for delivery of the digital good is 1 NXT, with 2 NXT additional fee for each 32 bytes of encrypted data after the first 32 bytes. Descriptions and encrypted delivery data size limit is 1000 bytes.

At present, the Nxt Marketplace remains an almost undiscovered secret, ready to be put to wider use. It is being used through the Nxt Client, but the Marketplace feature can easily be made the backbone of an app store, a decentralised crypto exchange, a subscription-based payment system for journalists, musicians or game developers, even a full-featured decentralised global auction site. Only the imagination of the developer – or the business ordering the use case – sets the limits. The low fees and uncensored decentralised nature of the Marketplace mean that it can solve real problems in any kind of market.

A decentralised and unregulated marketplace can attract people seeking to circumvent the laws of their country, this can not be prevented. But 3rd party websites can be made to filter listings according to their local laws. The current solution is to be on your guard, preferably only deal with people you know, always do your due diligence (read their customers' feedback) and, if possible, use a trusted escrow[1] for larger transactions. There is no built-in escrow or reputation system in the Nxt core (Nxt Reputation System is a feature planned for a future release). Clients or websites could however implement a solution like CONCORDE[2], or use Nxt

---

1 https://en.wikipedia.org/wiki/Escrow
2 https://nxtforum.org/freemarket/ann-concorde

Phased transactions[3] to set up an escrow service.

3 More information in the chapter: 'Phasing transactions'.

NXT

a revolutionary tool for businesses

NXT Cryptocurrency

NXT - A REVOLUTIONARY TOOL FOR BUSINESSES

Written by: Roberto 'Capodieci' Capodieci[1]

"At the moment, the 'blockchain' is a buzz word and every financial institution thinks it needs to have a project involving one, even if in most cases they have not much idea of what it means. And, at the other end of the supply chain – the end users – don't even know what they are using. I recently overheard someone expressing his surprise that to use Facebook he needed an Internet connection: to him, Facebook was an application on his phone, and had nothing to do with the Internet.

As with any new technology there is a huge need for education in order to gain adoption."

~ Capodieci

Early business success

I was born in 1974, one of the first generation of acne-ridden, computer-loving geeks. At school I learned to write in my (paper) notebook and, at home, to write code on my computer keyboard. I began my IT entrepreneurial career when I was still in my teens. By the age of 20 I was running an office with almost 40 developers and

---

1 Roberto is an Italian blockchain expert and entrepreneur; CEO at OTDocs, CTO at Digital Billions Pte Ltd, founder of MagniSign and DeBuNe (the Decentralised Business Network).

software engineers. My business partner, who covered the creative aspect of our business was a talented illustrator and graphic designer, with a passion for comic books and video games.

We had the usual joint signature controlled bank account and an ATM card with a monthly withdrawal limit which we used as a way to con-trol our expenditure. Trust was a necessary condition for our success: trust of each other and of the people and institutions we relied on for our business: the bank, the phone company, the accounting firm, our suppliers, and our clients.

Human-based problems

Money was pouring in, and things were getting better and better. But unfortunately it wasn't long before jealousy and resentment sprung up and started poisoning our working relationships. Trust in other people, so essential to the continuing success of our conventionally operated business model, started to fade away and then one day vanished completely following various incidents of dishonesty.

From fake accounts of who did what or who said what to whom, to actual fake accounting, my dream come true of running a successful IT business had now become a nightmare. Somehow my business partner managed to get some company cheques paid even though they had been signed only by him, leaving the company with a huge debt with the bank, and consequently with suppliers and those who were working with us.

Our successful business, which had lasted 7 years, was now effectively finished.

What had gone wrong?

The fundamental problem was inherent and, at the time, irremediable: we were, of necessity rather than choice, still living in a world of corruptible paper-based information and rule enforcement which was wholly dependent on human honesty and competence rather than mathematics.

So it was that the bank had failed to respect our agreement with them (paying cheques only if signed by both company directors), simply because it was up to a human to decide if that rule should have been enforced or not. The company's viability was further compromised by the inevitable gossip, whose pernicious effect was made worse by false information which in practice was impossible to refute, given the absence of a public repository of digitally signed declarations.

After such a traumatic experience, I have since lived by the rule that, for me, "the ideal number of business partners is an odd number lower than 3" (i.e. 1).

Pre-blockchain solutions
(email and PGP signatures)

I dreamt of a future where it was no longer necessary to have to trust third parties in matters of business. A future where there was no need to guess if a signature had been forged or not, where I could rest easy knowing that nobody could steal from the company's bank account, a future where if an agreement was made, it would be respected no matter what.

Such were my dreams during the first years of the Internet; years that were characterized by the slow and noisy dial-up modems that I had previously used only to connect to BBS or packet networks.

Email technology, as well as providing us with the convenience of near-instant written communication, effectively moved agreements away from being exclusively recorded on paper (or thermal fax paper) to being recorded in a searchable set of digital data, with timestamps and a sort of guarantee as to the identity of the originating party. I could now say: „Hey, this is what we agreed on such and such a date. Check your emails".

Then came the PGP signature: cryptographic certification that the content of an email hadn't been tampered with by someone with access to the mail server. I loved it. I loved emails for their federated network structure. There wasn't a unique central Mr Mail authority, but a network of many mail servers, each serving a portion of the total email users.

DeBuNe - a solution
in search of a technology to deliver it

It was the success (albeit limited) of the 'pre-blockchain solutions' that gave me the idea for what turned out to be DeBuNe[2] but, at the time, the technology needed to give effect to DeBuNe (i.e. the blockchain) didn't exist.

I used to think to myself: if only each mail server in this federated network had a copy of all the emails ever sent, then yes, we would have a replicated dataset and nobody could cheat, either regarding an email's contents, or its metadata: who sent it, at what date and time, etc. If I sent an invoice to my client, and he replied with a promise of payment and that information was unchangeable and digitally signed, then there could be no possible dispute as to what had been agreed.

Some of my other more wild imaginings included: if only my client could have sent me the payment via email...If only contracts to hire people and the salary agreements were supported by a network of servers, similar to those used for emails, but specifically for legal documents and financial agreements... I could then use such a network to manage my company, do away with the need for banks, seal agreements with my partner and the people working with me, set up special contracts regulated by software which managed the financial and decision flow automatically, all with the agreement of

---

2 Whitepaper: http://debune.org/DeBuNe.pdf. Video presentation: https://youtu.be/hGpgYWP4DNw

the parties involved being irrevocably and irrefutably evidenced by their digital signatures...

Bitcoin: a ground-breaking step in the right direction

When Bitcoin came out, I must have been among the first to cry 'Eureka', not so much for the cryptocurrency, but for the blockchain - this was a simple yet awesome solution to the decentralisation problem. I saw here the possible beginnings of that network for legal agreements and financial flows I had been dreaming of ever since human fallibility had put an end to my early business success.

However, while I find very romantic and amazing the algorithms and logic of Bitcoin's blockchain technology and how it has made decentralisation a practicable reality, I don't approve of the PoW approach (which is a waste of electricity and computer power). Moreover, the Bitcoin blockchain was designed purely as a ledger of financial remittances, it is not structured to support the far bigger data sets that DeBuNe needs in order to operate[3].

---

3 DeBuNe is a technological implementation, built on a fork of Nxt's NRS (aka node software or core), that decentralises business processes so that multiple parties can work together trustlessly. The key components include:
-digital identities, with digital signatures
-relative distributed KYC mechanics (for example the project magnisign. com is a spin off from DeBuNe.org to safely manage digital signatures)
-decentralisation thanks to the blockchain
-form editor and workflows designer to manage business processes
DeBuNe technology is used for FinTech solutions such as OTDocs.com.

Nxt - the complete decentralised business solution

I had to find a blockchain based solution that did more than just financial transactions.... and after some searching I found exactly what I was looking for: Nxt. DeBuNe.org (the Decentralised Business Network) could now finally see the light of day.

Nxt really is a revolutionary tool for businesses - one that has more than I could ever have hoped for!

Specifically:
- the good old email (called messaging), with the additional plus that each message is digitally signed and timestamped simply by belonging to a precise block height. Messages can be private (encrypted), or public, so that everyone can see the agreement between two parties;
- a marketplace, where the buyers and sellers of goods and services can be completely confident in the enforceability of the agreement between them, including all the steps needed to help deliver the goods, offer a discount, or reimburse the buyer;
- a voting system to allow a company taking decision and giving voice to both employees and clients;
- a monetary system to create tokens or credit or currencies to be used for many different needs in both organising, authorising, and controlling business processes;
- an asset exchange that offers the opportunity to the wide pub-

lic to invest in a business and trade assets in an open market;

- the possibility to store in the blockchain, for a definite or indefinite amount of time, small files, images, or other media;
- an alias directory that works as DNS or even contact lists;
- a tool to digitally sign text and data, respecting the digital identity in the blockchain, and yet useable outside the blockchain!
- and, last but definitely not least, it has the capacity to implement and install plugins, for custom needs and expanded uses.

Nxt is indeed the most amazing decentralised tool for businesses that knows no borders, no central authorities, no risks of fraud. With its API and hundreds of endpoint calls, Nxt is an easy tool to integrate with other software solutions, thus being the perfect solution for each business need. And furthermore, Nxt already has an almost 3 year 100% stable and reliable operational track record and that's all the trust that's needed.

If only it had been invented 25 years ago.

Editor's note: DeBuNe did a crowdfunding on Nxt AE in early 2015 to fund its initial work. Later in 2015 it went through a startup accelerator[4], and have since applied its technology to several use cases to have an income while implementing it. Roberto writes, "legally there is no connection between the AE of the Nxt blockchain and DeBuNe the legal company incorporated in Singapore. I (must) clarify this important aspect, as it is not legal in Singapore (and pretty much everywhere on the planet) to represent company

---

[4] https://cointelegraph.com/news/singapore-govt-backed-finttech-accelerator-boosts-3-bitcoin-startups

shares outside the governative provided registry". Naturally, and like all other legally registered businesses on the AE, Roberto would like regulators to catch up with modern technology.

NXT

monetary system

NXT Cryptocurrency

MONETARY SYSTEM

Written by: apenzl, Cassius

Nxt's Monetary System (MS) was activated at block height 330000, on January 10th, 2015.

The Monetary System is an innovation that allows people to design and issue new, off-the-peg cryptocurrencies, using the Nxt block-chain to secure it, rather than bootstrapping a whole new network, thereby removing a major impediment to easy, real-world adoption and use of different customised cryptocurrencies. New coins are highly customisable, with a wide range of parameters that can be set to govern their properties and use.

It is possible to launch an MS coin that is distributed by a Proof-of-Work-like mining mechanism, but secured by Nxt's PoS algorithm. It is possible to create fiat- and commodity-backed tokens for particu-lar real-world applications, allowing the creation of niche currencies for highly specific applications, like crowdfunding coins, 'regular' altcoins, reward points, coins pegged to fiat currencies or precious metals, this without going through the trouble of bootstrapping the currency with its own blockchain and network, while also being a stepping stone to new possible Nxt features, such as p2p loans, meaning that Nxt in effect can become the underlying tech for a completely decentralised banking system.

The issuance fee is based on the length of the currency code. A 5 letters code costs 40 NXT, a 4 letters code costs 1000 NXT, and a 3 letters code 25000 NXT. After the currency issuance, all other currency transactions (as of today) have a fee of only 1 NXT.

MS currencies are based on Nxt and therefore require NXT transaction fees[1].

Currency Properties

The currency type controls the inner workings of the currency. The full list of parameters which can be set for MS currencies includes[2]:

- **EXCHANGEABLE:** Currencies can be exchanged all within the NXT platform or on traditional exchanges, each identified by unique name and ticker symbols (e.g. BTC, USD).
- **CONTROLLABLE:** Currencies may optionally only be traded with the issuing account (e.g. backed tokens such as gift vouchers).
- **RESERVABLE:** Currency units are released and distributed if funding requirements are met within the given timescale, if not funds are automatically returned (e.g. crowdfunding).
- **CLAIMABLE:** Reserveable units can later be exchanged at an agreed rate.

---

1 NautilusCoin (NAUT), a cryptocurrency that was ported to Nxt, deals with this issue through a dedicated wallet that deducts fees in NAUT automatically, taking care of the conversion to NXT behind the scenes.
2 More detailed information about properties, can be read on: https://bitbucket.org/JeanLucPicard/nxt/issue/205/monetary-system-documentation

- **MINTABLE:** Currencies can be mined by proof-of-work algorithms (SHA-256, SHA-3, Scrypt and keccak), whilst still being secured by NXT's proof-of-stake algorithm.
- **NON_SHUFFLEABLE:** This property indicates that this currency cannot participate in coin shuffling. By default currencies are allowed to participate in shuffling[3].

Properties can be mixed and matched in various ways to compose the currency type.

The total currency supply is divisible into currency units. Currency units support decimal positions implemented as a client side feature. The maximum number of currency units which can be issued per currency is similar to NXT: i.e. $10^9 * 10^8$. The actual maximum units supply is set by the currency issuer. The issuer is responsible for setting the currency properties and in some configurations has additional control over the currency usage.

Currency Exchange

Nxt has a built-in exchange, where users can see all currency exchange offers (intuitively similar to fiat exchange offices) and match them with buy/sell exchange requests. This exchange is available from the Nxt Client, and a list of all issued currencies and their exchange offers can be found on blockchain explorers, such as nxtportal.org/currencies and mynxt.info/currencies/?all.

---

3 You can learn about the Shuffling feature in the chapter 'Shuffling your way to privacy'.

Editor's note: All Nxt MS currency names and codes will be ported to Nxt 2.0 first childchain[4], including currency balances for all accounts.

In addition, the Nxt Core Development Team will provide support to any MS currencies that want to transition to a Nxt 2.0 childchain, i.e. start a childchain with a token distribution based on this MS currency. MS currencies themselves are universal, and will be possible to trade on any childchain[5].

---

4 For more information about Nxt 2.0 and childchains, see the chapter 'Nxt 2.0; ARDOR'.
5 Source: https://nxtforum.org/core-development-announcements/announcing-nxt-2-0-roadmap

The Regulatory Process:

if you're not at the table,
you're on the menu

 NXT Cryptocurrency

THE REGULATORY PROCESS: IF YOU'RE NOT AT THE TABLE, YOU'RE ON THE MENU

by Robert Bold, Kushti, Jean-Luc and Riker. Many thanks to mthcl and ChuckOne who reviewed and commented on the article.

On 22nd April 2015 The European Securities and Markets Authority ('ESMA')[1], the equivalent of the US Securities and Exchange Commission, issued a call for evidence[2] regarding 'Investment using virtual currency or distributed ledger technology'.

Nxt is the example of the digital currency platform ESMA used in its 'call for evidence' to illustrate how distributed ledger technology works.

ESMA has published[3] the 18 responses it received, only two of which were made on behalf of cryptocurrencies: Nxt and FIMK (which is based on the Nxt blockchain). No response was made on

---

1 ESMA states on its website that it:
'...is interested in how different virtual currencies and the associated blockchain, or distributed ledger, can be used in investments. There are now facilities available to use the blockchain infrastructure as a means of issuing, transacting in and transferring ownership of securities in a way that bypasses the traditional infrastructure for public offer and issuance of securities, trading venues like exchanges and central securities depositaries or other typical means of recording ownership. ESMA would like to find out more about these market developments and in particular to know to what extent the use of the blockchain could enter the financial mainstream, and how it could be used.'
2 https://www.esma.europa.eu/sites/default/files/library/2015/11/2015-532_call_for_evidence_on_virtual_currency_investment.pdf
3 https://www.esma.europa.eu/press-news/consultations/investment-using-virtual-currency-or-distributed-ledger-technology

behalf of Bitcoin, although one was made in support of it by an exchange called Paymium.

No response to the ESMA call for evidence was made on behalf of (or even in support of) Ethereum, Counterparty, MaidSafe etc.

One can of course understand the lack of engagement on the part of the majority of cryptocurrencies (being, as they mostly are, opportunistic Bitcoin clones), but for Bitcoin itself and other serious players such as those mentioned above not to have responded is surprising.

The cryptocurrency industry needs to fully engage in the regulatory process to make sure that the potential for independent, genuinely decentralised, blockchain technology to democratize financial power is not compromised by a failure to challenge incompleteness or other inaccuracy in the information relied on by regulators.

Some examples of incompleteness and other inaccuracies can be found in the following extract of the ESMA response from Intesa Sanpaolo (a banking group based in Italy):

> "We would like to point out that, unlike Bitcoin's Proof of Work method (which, as stated in O1, we regard as the only effective one, at least at the moment, because of the computational power dedicated to it), other decentralized double-spending prevention algorithms, like NXT's Proof of Stake (PoS) presented in paragraph n.17, are still not validated from both a theoretical and an empirical point of view:

- *There is an ongoing debate over the "Nothing at Stake" problem affecting every system which doesn't use any consumption of resources external to the system for the validation;*
- *Every single existing PoS scheme, NXT included, is actually relying on some kind of centralization in validation checkpoints, in "currency" ownership or in nodes distribution."*

It would not of course be reasonable to expect a mainstream commercial banking group to argue in favour of a genuinely independent decentralised financial ecosystem.

Rather, it is for the proponents of that technology to correct any inaccuracies and supply any omissions in how others (doubtless unintentionally) represent it, but to do that they need to get involved in the consultation process.

Thus, by way of correcting certain inaccuracies and otherwise filling in the gaps, we shall deal with each of Intesa's three claims in turn.

Intesa Sanpaolo claims that Bitcoin's Proof of Work (PoW) method has been empirically and theoretically validated and that Nxt's Proof of Stake (PoS) method has not.

Theoretically, the PoW and PoS consensus mechanisms are neither better nor worse than each other, merely different. For a description of Nxt's Proof of Stake model, see pages 5/6 of Nxt's Response to ESMA[4].

---

4 https://www.esma.europa.eu/file/12959

As regards, the respective theoretical formalizations of PoW and PoS, the following points should be noted:

PoW formalization

The initial Satoshi Nakamoto paper (Bitcoin: A Peer-to-Peer Electronic Cash System[5]) only investigated the consensus algorithm security against private branch attack.

Since then other potential attack vectors, for example selfish mining[6], have been discovered.

The selfish mining strategy provides unfair profit for the 33+% adversary and that's dangerous in the long-term, but not critical for consensus itself.

Most recently, in November 2014, the formal model (of a more or less appropriate quality) was published: The Bitcoin Backbone Protocol: Analysis and Applications[7].

PoS formalization

Whilst Proof-of-Stake formalization is currently still behind that of PoW it's now developing faster than PoW's formalization and therefore catching up quickly.

5 http://nakamotoinstitute.org/bitcoin
6 http://arxiv.org/abs/1311.0243
7 http://courses.cs.washington.edu/courses/cse454/15wi/papers/bitcoin-765.pdf

The first implementations of pure PoS appeared in the second half of 2013, with the first investigations started in the first half of 2014 (Math of Nxt Forging[8] by mthcl) following which Consensus Research[9] made simulations[10] and wrote articles[11] about the few types of known attacks.

Consensus Research are currently in the process of discussing deeper formalization with colleagues from mathematics and theoretical computer science.

Turning next to Intesa Sanpaolo's claim that Bitcoin's PoW method has been "empirically validated" and that Nxt's PoS method has not.

We assume "empirically validated", as applied to Bitcoin's PoW and Nxt's PoS technologies, is intended to mean: proven to work in practice in accordance with their objectives.

Since both technologies demonstrably do work in practice in accordance with their objectives, at least up until now, they can therefore both be said to have been empirically validated: Bitcoin as a payment system and Nxt as a financial ecosystem which includes a payment system (see: Nxt Core Features, as described on pages 15/16 of Nxt's response to ESMA[12]).

But blockchain technology in general is still in its infancy and faces

---

8 https://www.docdroid.net/ecmz/forging0-5-2.pdf.html
9 http://consensusresearch.org
10 https://github.com/ConsensusResearch/ForgingSimulation
11 https://github.com/ConsensusResearch/articles-papers
12 https://www.esma.europa.eu/press-news/consultations/investment-using-virtual-currency-or-distributed-ledger-technology

a number of significant practical challenges, including that of block-chain bloat and scalability – a problem which, at some stage, will have to be addressed and resolved (if they are to remain viable) by all blockchain technologies, including of course Nxt itself.

However, due to the large and (as currently anticipated) increasing number of transactions being processed through its network, Bitcoin now needs to address that problem as a matter of urgency and it is running out of time in which to do so.

According to Bitcoin Foundation Chief Scientist Gavin Andresen speaking in an interview[13] in June 2015, Bitcoin will be reaching its 1 MB block size limit "some time in the next 6 to 12 to 18 months....". In the interview Mr Andresen goes on to warn of what could happen if the problem isn't resolved[14].

In an apparent attempt to force the pace as regards tackling the block size issue, a patch to the Bitcoin Core was released on August

---

13 https://www.youtube.com/watch?v=KYWhShzzELg
14 In the interview (at 6:43 mins), Bitcoin Foundation Chief Scientist Mr Andresen, who has a less apocalyptic vision than his colleague Mike Hearn as to what might happen to Bitcoin in a worst case scenario, nevertheless warns that:
"...people will just stop sending transactions if they notice that their transactions are not getting confirmed in a day or two or three or a week. The nature of transaction confirmation and the nature of how blocks are found softens that a little bit so every once in a while we'll get a period of time when transactions really pile up because blocks are found more slowly than normal and every once in a while we'll have a period of time where lots of transactions get confirmed because we're finding lots of blocks.
It's just the nature of the randomness of mining that we get this natural variation in how many transactions are confirmed in any given period of time and so I think that that natural variation plus people react so if you're sending transactions with very low fees that aren't getting confirmed well then you'll bump up your fees if you can and if you can't bump up your fees because transactions get more expensive then you find some alternative and that alternative may be: well I won't use Bitcoin, I'll find some other way of doing what I want to do.
So I don't think we'll have a crash. It won't be a disaster. I think what we will see is people turning away from Bitcoin and using other things and I think we'll see transaction fees rising. Both of these things I think are bad."

4th and is now available to download here: https://bitcoinxt.soft-ware/

It remains to be seen whether the Bitcoin network as a whole will accept or reject what in effect is a hard fork or indeed whether the network will split, resulting in the creation of two versions of Bitcoin, thereby crashing the value of one, if not both.

What is certainly clear is that the Bitcoin XT debate (whether or not to replace the current hard-coded block size limit of 1mb with a patch that, amongst other things, supports larger blocks) has polarized opinion[15].

And it is doing so for the reason explained in this article in The Wall Street Technologist:

"What we have here is an ideological schism in Bitcoin. Most people fail to realize that this is what the block debate is really about. On one hand you have folks who believe Bitcoin should be the new VISA system. They believe that Bitcoin should be able to handle all the transactions on planet earth, from everyone's daily coffee purchase, to everyone's house purchase, to how Google cars should be paid for their services. On the other hand, you have those who believe Bitcoin's

---

15 http://www.wallstreettechnologist.com/2015/08/19/bitcoin-xt-vs-core-blocksize-limit-the-schism-that-divides-us-all/: "The news recently is all abuzz about the Gavin Andresen and Mike Hearn's fork of Bitcoin called Bitcoin XT. For the first time in the history of Bitcoin, its very existence has been put into peril by way of what is termed a 'Hard Fork' of the protocol. I have watched the situation develop, and I feel that I must comment on this topic as the amount of FUD coming from both sides of the camps is reaching alarming levels, and frankly I think this is hurting Bitcoin."
As at 24 November 2015, there were 410 Bitcoin XT nodes (supporting bigger blocks) out of a total of 5018 nodes in the Bitcoin network. Source: http://www.xtnodes.com / Accessed 24.11.2015.

core value is the fact that it is a hedge against fiat currencies, and by extension, governments (in the case they decide to infringe upon your liberties). Bitcoin CANNOT be both. It's just not possible."

Whilst, as already mentioned, the scalability problem is common to all blockchain technologies, the following empirically observed problems are exclusive to Bitcoin and should also be borne in mind when reassessing the accuracy of any claim that Bitcoin is empirically valid:

- the inherent tendency of the underlying economics of the Bitcoin network to create a vicious circle whereby increasingly sophisticated mining rigs generate increased hash output resulting in increased difficulty which in turn drives the need for evermore powerful rigs thereby making it uneconomic for any but the biggest miners and pools to operate. The end result: increasing centralisation of mining power; i.e. a shrinking network of nodes, making it less secure[16].

- over-dependency on a few manufacturers of the prohibitively

---

16 "As a Proof of Work network becomes stronger, there is less incentive for an individual peer to support the network, because their potential reward is split among a greater number of peers. In search of profitability, miners keep adding resources in the form of specialized, proprietary hardware that requires significant capital investment and high ongoing energy demands. As time progresses, the network becomes more and more centralized as smaller peers (those who can do less work) drop out or combine their resources into pools." Source: http://wiki.nxtcrypto.org/wiki/Whitepaper:Nxt#Proof_of_Stake_Attacks
See also:
"The risk is that the trend will claim too much obsolete hardware and put many miners out of business, resulting in even more centralisation and fewer incentives to invest in the mining space." Source: http://www.coindesk.com/bitcoin-mining-can-longer-ignore-moores-law
And:
"The problem is that there is little incentive to run a node anymore. That's because powerful machines built specifically for bitcoin's SHA-256 proof-of-work algorithm have changed its decentralized and more open nature. Source: "http://www.coindesk.com/five-biggest-threats-facing-bitcoin

expensive ASIC mining equipment.

- high energy consumption involved in miners competing for blocks to validate, making the process environmentally very unfriendly.

Intesa Sanpaolo claims that "there is an ongoing debate over the "Nothing at Stake" problem affecting every system which doesn't use any consumption of resources external to the system for the validation."

The unqualified use of the word "problem" might suggest to the uninformed reader that Nxt, as a PoS system, has actually been subjected to a Nothing-at-Stake attack. In fact, it has not.

Like Bitcoin's PoW, the Nxt PoS consensus algorithm is a work in progress; the current state of thinking and research regarding any theoretical vulnerability to a N@S attack can be summarised as follows:

A. The first more or less formal definition (at least in the form of computer code) has been produced by Consensus Research: 'PoS forging algorithms: multi-strategy forging and related security issues'[17].

B. The number of possible forks grows exponentially over time. A Nothing-at-Stake attack could therefore only be made by a multi-branch forger contributing to N best forks and since it's impos-

---

[17] https://github.com/ConsensusResearch/articles-papers/blob/master/multi-strategy/multistrategy.pdf

sible to predict whether 2 forks will be within N best forks from the exponentially growing set for k confirmations (a significant imponderable), this attack vector is inherently unpredictable making it very difficult to enforce in theory, let alone in practice.

C. The correlation with stake size is still the open question but, contrary to what has been stated by Vitalik Buterin[18], it's nearly impossible to attack a proof-of-stake currency with "1% stake even".

D. A solution to make the PoS consensus algorithmically enforced (as in PoW) is theoretically possible.

---

18 Vitalik Buterin is one of the original authors of a cryptocurrency platform called Ethereum. A version of Ethereum, called Serenity, currently in development "... is meant to move from consensus through Proof-of-work to Proof-of-Stake." Source: https://blog.ethereum.org/2015/08/01/introducing-casper-friendly-ghost/
The "Nothing at Stake" attack is described by Vitalik Buterin:
"However, this algorithm has one important flaw: there is "nothing at stake". In the event of a fork, whether the fork is accidental or a malicious attempt to rewrite history and reverse a transaction, the optimal strategy for any miner is to mine on every chain, so that the miner gets their reward no matter which fork wins. Thus, assuming a large number of economically interested miners, an attacker may be able to send a transaction in exchange for some digital good (usually another cryptocurrency), receive the good, then start a fork of the blockchain from one block behind the transaction and send the money to them selves instead, and even with 1% of the total stake the attacker's fork would win because everyone else is mining on both." Extract from https://blog.ethereum.org/2014/11/25/proof-stake-learned-love-weak-subjectivity
In the following two papers, the authors also seek to prove the feasibility of a "Nothing at Stake" attack "It Will Cost You Nothing to 'Kill' a Proof-of-Stake Crypto-Currency" Nicolas Houy, University of Lyon, January 2014 (http://papers.ssrn.com/sol3/papers.cfm?abstract_id=2393940).
"On Stake and Consensus", Andrew Polesta, March 2015 (https://download.wpsoftware.net/bitcoin/pos.pdf)
By contrast, here's a detailed description, written in layman's terms, on the practical impossibility of N@S attack by JordanLee:
http://www.peercointalk.org/index.php?topic=2976.msg27303#msg27303
Discussion threads regarding the theoretical possibility of a Nothing-at-Stake attack include:
Nothing-at-Stake & Long Range Attack on Proof-of-Stake (Consensus Research): https://bitcointalk.org/index.php?topic=897488.msg10152632#msg10152632)
The Paper on Long-Range attack & Nothing-at-Stake: https://nxtforum.org/consensus-research/the-paper-on-long-range-attack-nothing-at-stake/msg141517/
NXT Sub-Forum: Consensus Research: https://nxtforum.org/consensus-research

E. The N@S simulation tool is published here: https://github.com/ConsensusResearch/MultiBranch for people to carry out their own experiments. Unfortunately, there is not currently any easy-to-understand (i.e. non-technical) visualization of the non-feasibility of a Nothing-at-Stake attack.

In practice, the Nxt forging algorithm provides a defence against a Nothing-at-Stake attack in the form of what has been termed Transparent Forging (TF)[19], the main feature of which is the ability to predict which account will generate the next block.

Other TF aspects of the Nxt forging algorithm are:

- account balance having to be older than 1440 blocks;
- the ability to lease account balance for forging;
- requiring the forging account to have had its public key announced for 1440 blocks before being able to forge; and,
- not accepting a forged block if its timestamp is more than 1 second after the predicted time to forge.

Improvements to take effect in release 1.7 are a minimum effective balance requirement of 1000 NXT for an account to be eligible to forge, and preventing very long blocks by an improved base target adjustment algorithm.

Elements of the TF concept which have not yet been implemented include: achieving higher transaction processing speeds by sending transactions directly to the node expected to generate the next

19 http://nxtwiki.org/wiki/Transparent_Forging

block, and reducing the time interval between blocks based on the knowledge of the next few predicted block generator accounts.

Further protection against any 'Nothing at Stake' attack can be achieved by temporarily reducing to zero the forging power of accounts which should have generated a block but skipped their turn. At present though, the currently implemented components of TF are considered sufficient to protect against such an attack.

Those TF elements mentioned above which are designed to increase the possible transaction throughput will only be implemented once the need for it appears, and certainly not until blockchain pruning has first been implemented.

Intesa Sanpaolo claims that "Every single existing PoS scheme, NXT included, is actually relying on some kind of centralization in validation checkpoints, in "currency" ownership or in nodes distribution."

At their current level of technological development, no blockchain (arguably Bitcoin least of all) is 100% decentralised.

Nxt validation checkpoints

The Nxt protocol includes a rolling checkpoint whereby any block submitted at a height more than 720 blocks behind the current block height is automatically rejected. This in effect limits chain reorganization to the most recent 720 blocks.

The Nxt protocol also includes some hard-coded checkpoints (e.g. at Block 333,000). Their purpose is to prevent any possibility of a so-called "history rewriting attack" in which somebody buys redundant early stakeholder accounts in order to try to build a complete alternative blockchain.

Another reason for the hard-coded checkpoints is performance optimization, specifically: improved blockchain download speeds for peers downloading the blockchain from scratch, the improved speed being due to the fact that they don't need to check with multiple peers in respect of the blockchain before the latest hard-coded checkpoint whether or not the current fork they are on is the best one.

Most importantly, such hard-coded checkpoints are only added at blocks more than 720 blocks before the current (at the time of adding the checkpoint) last block. At this point, the consensus has already been reached and set in stone by the rolling 720 block checkpoint limit, therefore the hardcoded checkpoint does not influence the decentralized consensus.

Whether or not these validation features can be regarded as "centralised" is debatable and in any case neither are critically needed for blockchain survival.

Bitcoin, of course, has its own hard-coded checkpoints (see further: https://github.com/bitcoin/bitcoin/blob/master/src/chainparams. cpp)

Nxt currency ownership and node distribution

Nxt does not rely, as a matter of technical design, on centralisation of currency ownership or node distribution and the authors of this article are unaware of any PoS model (or indeed any other block-chain consensus mechanism) that does.

Proof-of-stake must have a way of defining the next valid block in any blockchain. Selection by account balance would result in (undesirable) centralization, as the single richest member would have a permanent advantage. Instead, several different methods of selection have been devised.

Randomized Block Selection

Nxt uses a pseudo-random algorithm to predict the next block generator i.e. forger, by calculating a hash value which should be lower than a target value using the combination of the account stake, time since last block, signature of the previous block and the forger account public key. Since all these parameters are publicly available, each node can predict, with reasonable accuracy which account will forge the next block.

It might be that what Intesa Sanpaolo meant to say in its ESMA re-sponse[20] was that in certain PoS models a relatively small number of accounts are in practice currently responsible for the majority of the work of validating blocks and earning the transaction fees for

20 https://www.esma.europa.eu/file/12962

doing so.

In the case of Nxt the original distribution of the currency was made to the 73 subscribers who participated at the start and as a continuing, albeit slowly improving, legacy effect of that relatively small distribution, it is true to say that a large percentage of the Nxt currency has been owned by a relatively small number of account-holders.

Nxt critics have long sought to portray this as an inherent irremediable weakness of the system. It is not and over time, as more people get involved in Nxt, the number of accounts will continue to increase and ownership become more diffuse.

In the meantime, having a large percentage of the currency concentrated in a relatively few hands has had some advantages for the system, not least of which is the relative absence of speculative manipulation (i.e. pump and dump) and the funding of development and marketing that would not have happened but for the generous bounties made available by large Nxt account holders.

Meanwhile, Proof of Stake blockchain technology, of which Nxt is the leading example, continues to innovate and improve.

The features implemented in the hard fork Release 1.7 include coin shuffling, account control for phased transactions (whereby an account is only allowed to submit phased transactions that require the approval of one or more other accounts), more stable block times and various usability enhancements.

Nxt core developers have added features that make it easier to use the platform in regulated financial environments, for example "account properties" which can be used to endorse accounts as having been verified or authorized by third parties (implemented in Release 1.7). A security enhancement, 2FA using hash chains, and "controllable assets", designed to satisfy legal requirements that only authorized accounts can purchase certain types of asset are planned for Nxt 2.0.

Acknowledgments:

Many thanks to kushti, Jean-Luc, Riker, mthcl and ChuckOne who all reviewed and variously commented on and contributed wording to the article.

NXT

shuffling your way to privacy

NXT Cryptocurrency

SHUFFLING YOUR WAY TO PRIVACY

Written by: apenzl

Transactions on the blockchain are transparent to everyone.

Coin Shuffling[1] is a privacy feature which enables users to mix their funds quickly and efficiently with other users' funds by creating a random mapping between the existing user accounts and new recipient accounts provided by the users. Coin shuffling can be used to perform mixing of NXT, MS currencies (unless created as non-shuffleable), and AE assets.

The Coin Shuffling feature has been active on the Mainnet since block 621000.

When you shuffle your coins, they will be sent to a new and never-before-used account (defined by you), and the coins will have no backstory. They will seem to have appeared out of nowhere. The more shufflers and the more shuffling of the same coins, the harder they will be to backtrack.

"The idea is that if you don't want other people to track some funds, for example salary, supplier invoices, birthday presents, the problem is that these transactions are written forever in the blockchain

---

 1 https://bitbucket.org/JeanLucPicard/nxt/issues/325/coin-shuffling

so if anyone ever finds your account address, for example when you pay for coffee at the cafeteria, then they can reconstruct your payment history and see that every month you get X NXT and deduce it's your salary or that you sent a transaction around the time of your wife's birthday and deduce how much you paid for her present. If instead you provide your employer every month a fresh new account address or several of them and your employer creates a shuffling when paying you, it will be much more difficult to deduce your salary in the future, since it would be dispersed over many un-linkable accounts".

~ Riker

The shuffling feature is based on an idea posted on Bitcointalk by Tim Ruffing[2] and his academic paper 'CoinShuffle: Practical Decentralized Coin Mixing for Bitcoin'[3] which is also the source of the feature name. Tim Ruffing has reviewed Nxt's implementation and rated it secure[4].

The Nxt client wallet provides user interface for users to monitor and coordinate their actions during the shuffling process. Any account can create a new shuffling, specifying the holding to be shuffled, the shuffle amount, number of participants required, and registration deadline. Shuffling can be performed using NXT, assets or MS currencies. With MGW coin-backed assets, where for example one SuperBTC represents exactly one Bitcoin, it is possible to also shuffle Bitcoins and any other MGW supported cryptocurrency

---

2 https://bitcointalk.org/index.php?topic=567625.msg6370451#msg6370451
3 http://crypsys.mmci.uni-saarland.de/projects/CoinShuffle/coinshuffle.pdf
4 https://nxtforum.org/core-development-discussion/coin-shuffling-code-review-by-tim-ruffing

in a fully decentralised way via the Nxt platform[5]. All that is required for the shuffling to be successful is from the shufflers to keep
their Nxt Client/nodes running through the shuffling process.

5 The MGW is a distributed gateway solution with which other digital currencies can
be sent to, and transferred from, the Nxt platform.

NXT

voting

NXT Cryptocurrency

VOTING

Written by: apenzl

Nxt includes a decentralised Voting System. You can create a poll concerning your project or company, and it will be sent to the asset holders (or whoever you want). The poll results will be collected automatically and ready to use, and the poll results are completely reliable. The result is instantly visible for all, as it is recorded in the blockchain.

Nxt Voting System was released with block 445000, on June 6th, 2015.

"Vote by asset, vote by account balance, vote by MS coin balance. You can do a yes or no, or a slider between values, like 1-10. The fun stuff comes with phased txs[1], after this you can make txs that depend on the result of a poll".

~ Jones

Consider the example of an indy developer making a game. First, he got some funds via the asset exchange. Then he made a promising first version of the game. Both the concept and its implementation are still raw but the fans are excited! So he wants to ask the community whether he should polish version 1 or instead build a version 2 on the basis of a better concept, or...? Having decided on the different options, he starts a poll.

---

1 To learn about automatically triggering transactions based on the voting result, see next chapter: "Phasing transactions".

With the Nxt Voting System any account can create polls with one question and up to 100 answers. Accounts are eligible to vote in the poll based on a minimum required balance of NXT, an asset, or an MS currency. An answer is given weight based on one of four voting models and then its weight is multiplied by the associated range value to compute a corresponding result. The four voting models specify weight as: one per voting account, or equal to the balance per voting account of NXT, or a specified asset or an MS currency[2].

Practical decision making

Nxters have tested and used the blockchain voting feature, as every other feature of Nxt, since its inception. Blockchain votes have been cast, to choose direction for the project, decide whether to back or dismiss Jean-Luc's proposal for the Nxt 2.0 design[3], when to start snapshots and distribute the new Nxt 2.0 (Ardor) tokens[4], other examples are voting in the NxtHacks 2015 hackathon[5], Super-NET voting how many percent of their holdings should be donated to the Iota Foundation[6], or the company Nxtty[7], which makes all its decisions based on their shareholders' votes; a pre-defined minimum amount of shares must be held in order to participate in the voting process (enabled by a smart transaction), and the poll results are of course public.

2 https://nxtwiki.org/wiki/Voting_System
3 https://nxtportal.org/polls/14844424216298754631, https://nxtportal.org/polls/8456081814557957525
4 https://nxtportal.org/polls/12536280419851201672
5 https://nxter.org/the-nxthacks-hackathon-2015/, https://nxtportal.org/polls/8316013305858322997
6 https://nxtportal.org/polls/6760910214030529023. Iota is a blockchain-less cryptocurrency created for micro-transactions for the Internet-of-Things, which can communicate with blockchains.
7 http://nxtty.com, http://www.newbium.com

E-proxy voting systems

In April 2016, Russia's central securities depository, (NSD), tested an e-proxy voting system based on the Nxt platform[8]. The NSD is a Russian non banking credit organization, Russia's central depository and a professional securities market player. The organization provides depository, banking settlement and "relevant services" to market players.

"It is obvious to us that ignoring the rapid development of FinTech and upgrading the outdated platforms could hinder the stable development of the Russian financial system", says Eddie Astanin, Chairman of the Executive Board of NSD. "Fortunately, Russian specialists are among the most experienced in the global FinTech industry, and we have proven this fact by implementing a fully functional prototype of e-proxy voting system based on [the Nxt] blockchain. After testing blockchain for bondholder meetings, we can extend the use of this technology to other business areas of NSD". The e-voting solution was developed in partnership with DSX Technologies, a distributed ledger technology company based in the U.K. According to Mike Rymanov, founder and CEO of DSX Technologies, blockchain technologies such as Bitcoin and Ethereum couldn't meet the project's requirements with an out-of-the-box solution, which motivated the choice of the Nxt Platform[9].

"Using the proof-of-work (PoW) Bitcoin blockchain would have potentially created a situation where a particular node with a superior

8 Poll: https://www.nsd.ru/en/press/ndcnews/index.php?id36=628973
9 Source: https://bitcoinmagazine.com/articles/russia-s-national-settlement-depository-successfully-tests-blockchain-based-e-voting-system-1464198071

computing power could gain an unfair advantage over its peers, thus jeopardizing the security of the network and, if being a malicious actor, could rig the results of the vote," said Rymanov. "Furthermore, we see PoW systems as an unnecessary drain on resources in private permissioned blockchains. After careful consideration we selected Nxt," Rymanov says. "The proof-of-stake (PoS) blockchain has provided us with enough flexibility to architect a solution that is scalable, stable and with processing capabilities well within the range of NSD expectations".

Rymanov is persuaded that e-proxy voting could find applications in wider contexts, potentially including political elections. "The technology we have developed can potentially be used for general elections, providing transparency and enabling significant savings," he says. Sergey Putyatinskiy, IT Director of NSD, goes into further detail: "The distributed database for e-proxy voting contains a full update history, which is protected from tampering by cryptographic security. All members of the network (nominees and NSD) keep copies of the database, and in case of an inspection, the regulator or the auditor gets full access to all the necessary information simply by joining the network. Once data has been entered into the blockchain, it cannot be falsified: the system records all changes that have been made in the voting procedure or in the vote results stored in the distributed database. The record is then distributed among all the network members, and can easily be traced".

NXT

phasing transactions

 NXT Cryptocurrency

PHASING TRANSACTIONS

Written by: apenzl

Phasing was released with block 445000, on June 6th, 2015.

Nxt Phasing[1] is a feature that allows certain safe transactions to be created with conditional deferred execution based on the approval from 1-10 other accounts, the result of a vote, on a list of linked transactions or on the revelation of a secret; or simply with unconditional deferred execution (a transaction will automatically execute at a pre-set block height).

Phased transactions have been dubbed to be Nxt's implementation of multisig[2], but extend the definition of multisig to include many more functions and use cases. Most basically, a user is able to define a transaction in two phases: the first phase being when the details of the transaction are defined (for example the amount of NXT to send and the recipient), and the second being when the transaction is released into the system. Users can set multiple conditions before a transaction is executed. This greatly widens the range of possible use cases. For example,

1.   Joint accounts can be run with ease.
2.   Trustless escrow is possible by phasing two transactions in parallel.
3.   Asset holders can vote to veto or accept payments made by an

---

1 https://nxtwiki.org/wiki/Phasing
2 https://en.wikipedia.org/wiki/Multisignature

asset issuer or company on whose behalf the asset was issued.

Simplest example, Alice starts a Two-Phased transaction. In the first stage a transaction is included in the blockchain but it isn't processed immediately and has the status of 'pending'. For it to be processed, Bob has to complete the second phase of the transaction by approving it. This has to be done before the deadline set by Alice has elapsed. Approval can involve up to 10 pre-defined accounts or depend on the results of a poll.

Whitelist

A whitelist can be created with the inclusion of 1-10 accounts, so that only those accounts are eligible to approve a phased transaction or vote in the phasing poll. Whitelisted accounts receive an 'Approval Request', which is a mechanism for voting, when the phased transaction is created.

Approval by Vote

There are four voting models[3]:

- Vote by account
- Vote by account balance
- Vote by asset balance
- Vote by MS currency balance

---

3 For further details on Nxt's voting models, refer to the 'Voting System' chapter.

Additionally, there are also three balance models:

- Minimum balance of NXT required
- Minimum balance of asset quantity required
- Minimum balance of MS currency units required

The default selection is

- No minimum balance necessary (except 1 NXT for the transaction fee) meaning that possessing a minimum balance is not an eligibility requirement for voting.

Approval By Hash

A phased transaction can have a hash[4] attached to it. The first transaction must include the hash of a 'secret' chosen by the sender, and an approval transaction for it is only accepted if it includes the secret that results in this hash. It does not matter who the sender of the approval transaction is. If the approval transaction is received before the pre-set finish height, with an attachment containing the secret, the phased transaction will be automatically executed and if not, it will be reversed.

Two or more phased transactions can be set, depending on the same hash, which will be executed only if or when a transaction is received that contains the secret which matches that hash. This can be extended to up to 10 transactions being released with the

4 https://en.wikipedia.org/wiki/Cryptographic_hash_function

same secret, as a single approval transaction can approve up to 10 phased transactions, as long as the same secret is used.

Approval By Hash can be used to create cross-blockchain transactions with other blockchains that support the same method, as long as the same hash function is used. The currently supported hash functions are sha256, ripemd160, and sha256 followed by ripemd160[5].

Approval By Transaction

Finally, it is possible to make a phased transaction depend on the presence of other transactions in the blockchain; a transaction already in the blockchain before the acceptance of the phased transaction or a future transaction not yet in the blockchain. Such transactions can be created in advance and not broadcast. The signed transaction bytes must be broadcast later, before the finish height of the phased transaction, in order to approve it.

Up to 10 transactions can be linked to a pending phased transaction, which for example can be set to require at least n of them to be present in order to get approved and executed. Transactions of any type can be referenced, for example NXT transfers, asset transfers or MS transfers, as is the case with for example 'Quack'[6], a Nxt plugin offering atomic exchange of assets and Nxt MS coins directly without the need to convert them to NXT.

---

5 If there is a specific need, the Nxt core developers will extend this to support other hash functions.
6 Quack is an 'atomic transfer' Nxt plugin, for more info, see the chapter: 'Nxt Plugins'.

Account Control

Account Control for Phased transactions, when applied to an account, limits it to being used to submit phased transactions only. It is an additional level of security, so that even if the controlled account's passphrase (private key) is compromised, the assets are still safe.

The parameters of the voting model are fixed with the transaction that enables account control for the account, and can only be changed or removed with a transaction that is also phased, under the same voting model. If a vote on a transaction fails, then there is no way to override it.

NXT

the fork

NXT Cryptocurrency

THE FORK

Written by: apenzl

Nxt is great.... wouldn't you say? All that cutting edge tech, the new business models, intelligent decentralised community, forward-looking businesses. A glamorous tale of geeks changing the world with Java code, fighting scams in parallel with developing a disruptive platform for everybody. If only the world knew, everyone would be beating a path to our digital door.

That said....

Since this book wants to provide a 'snapshot' of both the Nxt software and ecosystem, from Genesis until now, it's appropriate to also deal with the downsides. And Nxt being a new technology, a social experiment, and at the same time a multi-million dollar (potential billion dollar) fintech project in development, there's certainly a selection of 'downsides' to choose from, some of which shook up the entire Nxt ecosystem. Yes, we've seen trolls. Lots of them. Scammers. We've seen people come and go, hackers trying to exploit the software, whales dumping, and also very potent social engineering happening inside the forums, but we've survived it all. Sometimes, in chats, we compare our bleeding wounds.

It has been said that BCNext handed over Nxt to the Nxt community. It's not the purpose of this chapter to point out scapegoats for unfortunate circumstances that have occurred in the past or point fingers at anyone whose conduct has given Nxt and Nxters a bad time.

An engine needs to be clean and well oiled and, as with software (Nxt included), necessary optimisations must be made from time to time. But exactly what 'necessary' means, depends on ones particular perspective, and back in 2015 there was a clash of core devs and 3rd party devs / Nxt Service Providers, which hurt the community far worse than all the asset scammers and hacking attacks combined.

Since the very beginning Jean-Luc has been lead developer of the core software, with a small team of developers helping him. Jean-Luc has from the start refused to be paid for his work, thus he can not be seen as an employee of the community. But while everyone can build 'on top' of the Nxt platform, only Jean-Luc can implement changes into the core.

What happens if a community, most of which is represented by a 3rd party developer, disagrees with the choices made by the software's lead developer, but both developers' arguments make sense?

We depend on each other, through ups and downs. This is the social experiment of Nxt.

"Bitcoin relies only on math, but math can't solve problems arising because of the illogical nature of the man. [Forging] in Nxt relies on

the cooperation of people, and even forces it. Without cooperation, Nxt becomes weak and can be easily attacked. It's like a system in unstable equilibrium. If people stop caring about cooperation, Nxt will fail very quickly."

~ BCNext

An asset [ANN]

jl777, a very active Nxt visionary, programmer and asset issuer, announced his SuperNetwork on Aug. 30 2014, just 7 days after announcing his 'Nxt Inside' initiative inside the Nxt forum[1]. The idea was to offer Nxt's 2.0 blockchain features to other existing crypto-coins, allowing them to benefit from the GUI, Asset Exchange and other aspects of Nxt's ecosystem, and extending the adoption of Nxt in the process - a mutually beneficial arrangement.

SuperNET would comprise the core tech developed by jl777, some revenue sharing core services, a 10% holding in all selected core coins, the SuperNET/UNITY asset and a bunch of promising part-nership projects. The owners of the SuperNET asset would earn revenue from all of this.

The SuperNET ICO (Initial Crowdfunding Offering[2]) campaign began on Saturday 6 September 2014, and in two hours 2000 BTC were raised. The ICO ended 16 days later, with a total of 5737.1589 BTC equivalent raised. It's worth noting the support given to SuperNET

---

1 https://nxtforum.org/general-discussion/price-speculation/msg90192/#msg90192
2 http://bitcoinist.net/just-what-the-heck-is-an-ico

by the Nxt Community who invested nothing less than 4.7 percent of NXT's total market cap (3715.3 BTC equivalent) in the SuperNET. The coins invested by participants at the ICO gave SuperNET its 'floor' value. But in addition to this, jl777 also added a large percentage of his own Nxt assets representing the SuperNET services in development. SuperNET though, was broadly analogous to a closed-ended mutual fund consisting of cryptocurrency balances, code, plus a series of revenue-generating services, built on top of Nxt.

The first public SuperNET BETA client was released in March 2015[3], as a MGW based multiwallet. The next groundbreaking feature to be implemented in it was InstantDEX.

> *"The goal of InstantDEX is to offer realtime trading of NXT, NXT assets and other cryptos. It will earn fees from commissions on the trades. By keeping costs low by using a decentralized infrastructure, it is expected to be able to distribute approximately half of revenues to asset holders".*
>
> ~ iDEX asset description, jl777[4]

"InstantDEX can be considered "the grand central station of Super-NET. It connects everything to everything else", James wrote, and on March 16, 2015 he announced:

> *"InstantDEX core API is feature complete other than auto-*

---

3 A centralised unit was enforced and paid to take care of the launch of the Super-NET beta client, a Nxt MultiGateWay-based multiwallet, which would convert selected altcoins into Nxt assets and thereby make them tradeable on the decentralised AE.
4 https://www.mynxt.info/asset/15344649963748848799

matching hybrid orderbooks. So now what is left is the most advanced case (hybrid orders), which isn't even necessary at first. (...) So, not quite 100%, but 99.99%+ with the downside being partial fills".

Good news. A 5% revenue share from SuperNET would go to NXT core development[5], and all InstantDEX fees were to be paid in NXT. As jl777 wrote: "At 50 trades per minute it saturates current NXT blockchain (makes NXT earn 10% per year), but NXT devs say they can boost this capacity pretty easily. With average fees of 6 NXT per trade that is 300K NXT per day or 15 million per month. So even at current ATH prices InstantDEX is trading at PS ratio of 5 and PE of 10".

Only problem: the asset price peaked but the release didn't happen.

"Go James!", cried the investors, "make us rich"! "Disrupt everything"!, contributed the anarcho-capitalists. jl777 was asking for testers, saying that without testers he couldn't find the bugs and fix them and prepare a public release, but his supporters did not have the time or expertise. jl777 had turned his attention to coding other parts of the SuperNET and "not being a GUI-dev", he was busy updating the MGW beta, coding new tech like RAMchains and Lchains, decentralised peggable crypto, a decentralised poker app, crypto777[6], and also issuing a new asset which represented shares in the hired SuperNET developers' future paychecks. But no further

---

5 SuperNET's official ICO paper was available here: http://209.126.70.170/SuperNET. pdf. It has been removed. Nxter.org has made a copy available here: https://nxter. org/supernet-ico-copy.pdf

6 http://www.digitalcatallaxy.com/report2015.html

ICO funds were being spent on progressing the client app.

Then, in May 2015, the SuperNET Newsletter revealed that: "James has been in deep coding mode, resulting in a total reconstruction of the SuperNET CORE[7]. The SuperNET is now a BTCD plugin"[8].

"I run the host code inside BTCD, and SuperNET plugs into it. I am focused on getting InstantDEX out, but need MGW stable and fast first. The modular agents' system solves the exponential increase in complexity of the overall project. These are things I didn't foresee and reliable decentralized networking is not as easy as it sounds".

~ jl777, May 2015

Tech fights

"They thought we were slaves and had no choice. Don't they realize who I am?"

~ jl777, February 2016[9]

Many Nxters had followed jl777 in his visions for Nxt and the SuperNET, and most discussions had moved from Nxt's forum to the SuperNET Slack, leaving the public Nxtforum almost silent. As the InstantDEX release date kept being postponed, and the pre-announced new tech, partnership launched and the expected massive dividend cashflow to SuperNET investors and fees to NXT forgers

---

7 Source: http://nxter.org/supernet-newsletter-17
8 BTCD (BitcoinDark) is an altcoin, for which jl777 was lead developer.
9 "Declaration of Independence": https://bitcointalk.org/index.php?topic=1372879.
msg13977621#msg13977621

didn't seem to materialize, the trolling began. jl777's c codebase grew, new ideas kept getting added, but no new features were added to the SuperNET client, no direct fiat > NXT gateway, no new core altcoins which integrated NxtInside or added their "special features" to the mix.

At the same time, due to a protracted bear market, most alt coins, including the NXT currency and the NXT AE market, suffered a long steady decline in price and trading volume. Asset issuers like Coino-mat was trying hard to revive the AE market but without success[10].

Nxt API changes

On April 11 2015, Jean-Luc released NRS v1.5.1e[11], an experimental release which introduced prunability of arbitrary data in the block-chain. Also, he proposed a new fee structure which would make it far more expensive to store larger amounts of data permanently in the blockchain. As one of the major uses of Nxt at the time was storing data via AMs (1000 bytes of storage for a 1 NXT fee), this naturally sparked discussions[12].

Among others, jl777 wanted to make sure that his services could keep on running with prunable messages on Nxt. It was confirmed. Other developers, who relied on Nxt's blockchain storage, announced that if the changes were implemented, it would actively break their Dapps.

---

10 See the chapter: Nxt - its history and potential, Crossing the desert
11 https://nxtforum.org/nrs-releases/nrs-v1-5-1e
12 https://nxtforum.org/nrs-releases/nrs-v1-5-1e/msg173829

The reasoning from the core developers was, that "we should stop thinking about the blockchain as **storage** space. When posting data to the blockchain (that are not related to its own functioning), what the blockchain should provide is **distribution** (after achieving the consensus on which transactions/data are accepted), and trustless future **verification** of this data. The storage part of it should shift to Service Providers[13]. Nodes can opt in to keep prunable data very long, even indefinitely. But the protocol should not force all the nodes to do it"[14].

"[NRS 1.5] will break compatibility, but we can't stick with a wrong decision forever".

~ Jean-Luc

And so, incompatible changes were included in the Nxt API.
And on October 31 2015, new API changes were made, with NRS version 1.6.2.

"Regarding the API change, rest assured that this decision was not taken lightly."

~ Riker

"1.6 is an optional upgrade, and this is why it is a good time to introduce incompatible changes, because those who need time to adapt to them can continue using 1.5 until ready. 1.7 [will be] a man-

---

13 Service Providers are those who provide services 'on top' of the Nxt core functionality. A service can for example be running an archival node, or a forging hub, but also shops, financial exchanges, decentralised email, etc, built on the Nxt platform. See http://www.nxttechnologytree.com: Service Providers will make possible the development of Distributed Computing, Distributed Storage, Global Collaboration and other future Nxt 2.0 features.
14 https://nxtforum.org/nrs-releases/nrs-v1-5-1e/msg173926

datory upgrade, because it is a hardfork. It is not good to postpone API changes until 1.7, because this allows users less time to update their code".

~ Jean-Luc

What Jean-Luc and the core development team had likely not expected, was the furore that was about to hit them - and the Nxt ecosystem.

The users of the official Nxt Client upgraded and started forging with the new version. Centralised NXT exchanges made the required changes and updated to NRS 1.6.2. And of course the public node operators updated and started running the new software version. But then all hell broke loose. Because as public nodes updated, some applications, including Jay (a 3rd party development framework built on top of Nxt), and also the MGW and the SuperNET Lite wallet[15], which was made to be dependent on "Jay"[16], broke.

jl777 reacted promptly in the release-thread on Nxtforum:

"Please fix all the websites that have been broken by this change. Please fix all the applications that have been broken by this change. Please test and validate all the changed websites and applications. Please restore the lost confidence of users that see terribly wrong results due to API change. (...)

---

15 https://nxtforum.org/nrs-releases/nrs-v1-6-2/msg199422/#msg199422
16 The SuperNET Lite client connected (via Jay) to random nodes in the network. Those nodes were expected to run the newest stable version of Nxt. So once the newest stable version (like 1.6.2) broke the API, SuperNET's apps did not function. Source: https://nxtforum.org/nrs-releases/nrs-v1-6-2/msg199257

tl:dr it is a MAJOR breach of trust as far as I am concerned that the API backward compatibility promise[17] has been violated and I cannot rely on NXT for any important SuperNET functions.

With this many changes and no direct communication, it is no surprise that everything broke. The local performance of API is not anything that should enable a CENTRALLY decided breaking of backward compatibility.

But there has been ZERO changes based on my feedback as I am not important enough to listen to. Neither are any of the other devs.

So I say goodbye

James

~ jl777[18]

The community was confused, stunned. Then the rage began. With all the stress already, WHY break backwards compatibility and lose developers and services? The SuperNET client was popular as a light client, and so was Jay's secure online version of the Nxt Client. Some users were quick to pick sides, not being tech-savvy, they only saw that their favourite Nxt Service was suddenly out of order and wanted to place the blame on somebody. Others, having respect for (and being invested in) both jl777 and Jean-Luc's great projects, were in a severe dilemma. Because the uncompromising

---

17 One year earlier, Jean-Luc had made incompatible changes in the Nxt core code to avoid an attack.
18 https://nxtforum.org/nrs-releases/nrs-v1-6-2/msg199227

tone between the developers was escalating, and now their fan-
boys contributed with their unresolved anger caused by the long
price dump.

"There will be no reversal in 1.6.3."

~ Jean-Luc

"guys I can see a direction where it all could go soon
current devs won't like it.
please stop doing such things, NXT DOES NOT belong to you".

~ Coinomat

"The first effect of all this is that ALL of my projects will be
delayed. I will wait for NXT API to stabilize before I waste my time. The
most likely scenario is that I will just remove all dependency on NXT
and put whatever functions I need into BTCD.

This breaking of API was done intentionally and the defaults for do-
zens of API calls REVERSED from what is already there. The fact this is
treated as a 'feature' and not a DOA bug boggles my mind. SuperNET
will incur a delay to remove its NXT dependency, but it will certainly not
die from not depending on NXT, rather my assessment is that it is more
likely to die if it depends on NXT that is guaranteed to not be backward
compatible"

~ jl777

It was a baptism of fire for TNNSE, who had just got funded by the

Nxt community. Jean-Luc had already posted his detailed explanation for the API changes in the forum[19], but to no positive effect. In a private Slack chat, Damelon, EvilDave, Nxt lead developers Jean-Luc and Riker, and later software engineer, a founding member of Nxt Foundation and SuperNET Service partner 'Chanc3r', tried to figure out a narrative for doing damage control and paving the best possible way forwards for Nxt and SuperNET[20]. Also, a mistake had been discovered, namely that default parameters had been changed from the last 'experimental' NRS version to the 'production ready' stable NRS 1.6.2 version release. Even though it was documented in the NRS 1.6.2 change-log, this was not best practice from Jean-Luc's side.

"It should have been called 1.6.2e, or the incompatible changes should have been in 1.6.1e, but this cat is out of the bag now. For the future, we commit to not making any incompatible changes between the last 'e' release and the subsequent stable release".

~ Jean-Luc

In a public summary, Dave 'EvilDave' Pearce wrote:

"This is a clear failure of the testing/review process for new Nxt releases, and we need to make some changes. Everyone involved wants to make sure that this sort of issue does not happen again in the future, and that no Nxt-based project is ever broken by an update of Nxt MainNet.

19 https://nxtforum.org/nrs-releases/nrs-v1-6-2/msg199197
20 Chat-log: https://drive.google.com/file/d/0B4OEA-peiYHXd3JOTUY4VndQLW8/view

SuperNET was probably the most affected by this issue, so I've spent some time to get feedback from jl777 on how he would like to move forward, and the core devs will be meeting most of his requests, but not all[21].

*The **API will not be rolled back** in a 1.6.3 release to the old 1.5.15 standard. The issues with 1.6.2 have been researched, understood and fixes have been implemented by most projects (ordinary desktop users are NOT affected, just to remind everyone). The 1.6 API changes are vital to allow Nxt to move to the 1.7 branch, and will have to be implemented in any case.*

*In order to ensure that there is a **clear line of communication** between Nxt core devs and external projects, we have set up an old-fashioned mailing list to allow a direct means of reporting bugs/requesting support/giving feedback from/to the core devs. This will be a massive improvement on the current forum-based communication.*

*Chanc3r has volunteered to lead on giving **SuperNET support** to help with any further issues that they may have, and the core devs are committed to helping everyone out with a smooth transition to 1.6.2.*

*The **review/testing process for major releases** will be changed. Bugfix/zeroday/patch releases will not be affected, but anything with an API change or a major new feature will have a compulsory review period of 2-4 weeks after release as an experimental version. In that time, the devs on the mailing list will examine and test the code to ensure that it*

---

21 The reasoning behind not committing to all jl777's requests, can be read by following the link in footnote 20.

functions in their production environment. (...)

Finding a balance between development and stability is what we need to do, and the best way to do that is to implement better change and release management for the Nxt core, and to improve communications between Nxt core devs and external project devs. Sign up for the mailing list, and start getting involved in this process.

~ EvilDave

The next day, Chanc3r followed up, representing someone with a foot in both camps:

"I did promise the TNNSE team I would post after long discussions yesterday, this is the first chance I have had.

The API change in 1.6.2 is minor, to adapt to it is simple, the addition of a single parameter to the calls, a grep of the application code reveals where these changes need to be done and they can be done in minutes, when the change is done API Calls to 1.5.15 and 1.6.2 BEHAVE IN EXACTLY THE SAME WAY.

I've looked at the Supernet code so I know the scope of the impact and changes, which while they take time to implement which would not have been planned they would not be far reaching in their impact. This is why I think this is evolving into an unnecessary power struggle between SuperNet and NXT.

If SuperNet uses public nodes and this is affected then unless those operators were to all upgrade to a 1.6.3 or Supernet is doing an explicit version compatibility check then the likelihood is Supernet components will still fail when they hit on an unmodified 1.6.2 node - hence I think a patch solves nothing if the Supernet code isn't changed because likely 1.6.2 will remain in service.

This has arisen because of a lack of realisation of these changes between the NXT team and the Supernet Team, during the release and testing process, nothing deliberate just a simple disconnect.

There has been acknowledgement from the NXT team that they need to communicate better in future and steps are underway to ensure this.

Unlimited backwards compatibility is not possible and NXT can't meet that for any user of the platform so NXT needs to get better at this and users of NXT need to be prepared to adapt in the time that is given to do so.

Is better legacy feature support necessary - yes and I think NXT realises this but this is still, relatively speaking, a young platform and there is room for improvement.

I appreciate the sudden breaking of Supernet on the release of 1.6.2 would have come as a shock, this was a simple error but simple also to fix. This was not an act of malice but a simple disconnect in the release / testing process and the simplicity to fix does not warrant some of the statements coming from the SuperNet team (my opinion, I'm sure others will disagree).

NXT is the operating system - it needs to develop and sometimes things will change that affect things that operate on top of this - does NXT need to be better at managing change impact - yes, I think this is understood and accepted and, as has been posted by the Foundation, steps will be put in place to approve this.

Regarding those calling for a vote - I disagree, most people won't know, care or more importantly understand what they are voting about. Also look at what the NXT platform is and its roadmap - this is the most important work of the developers and the future value of NXT.

We have a mob forming the requirement to add „includeAssetInfo=true" to the api call „getAccountAssets" and similar calls. Other platforms have confirmed they have already patched their API calls. I suggest we move on to more important things".

~ Chanc3r

The 1.6.2 API drama was intense for participants and readers, but now came a silence before the next storm. A path forward had been paved, and to some it made a lot of sense, but to others not. Nxt developers fixed the SuperNET applications. jl777 disappeared from Slack and Nxtforum. According to rumour he was in 'deep coding mode' making his project independent from Nxt, but no-one confirmed it.

The successful 1.7 hard fork showed that the majority of NXT stakeholders backed the further evolution of Nxt, but with the community split and long term Nxters feeling increasingly drained by years of unpaid work the overriding impression, exacerbated by troll attacks in the forum and chats, and people dumping both NXT and SuperNET, was one of uncertainty, doubt - and fear.

Then, shortly after, on February 8, 2016, Jean-Luc posted the core development team's vision for the next important step in Nxt's evolution.

The Nxt 2.0 design proposal

Nxt 2.0 would allow anyone to create their own childchain with Nxt, secure, light weight and customised for their needs, with its own transactional token, and at the same time the design aimed to solve the blockchain bloat problem, inherent in all existing blockchains, and thereby consolidate Nxt's position as a frontrunner in the blockchain 2.0 technology race.

But moving on to Nxt 2.0 (soon to be named 'Ardor'), would not be achieved simply by adding another set of features to the Nxt platform. It involved a much more radical change:

"The NXT token will be split into 'Ardor' and 'Ignis' tokens which together cover the same functions currently used by the NXT token. Ardor tokens will be used for forging, to maintain the network security and incentivize people to set up nodes. The first childchain, 'Ignis' (to be issued with the Ardor Genesis block) will initially be the transactional token of Nxt 2.0, until new child chains can be spawned. Ignis will be issued with the same features as Nxt 1.0, but be continuously developed

by the core team. NXT 1.0 will continue to exist".

~ Riker

Jean-Luc explained the reasons for the change:

"The Nxt development team is constantly acquiring feedback from businesses looking to use the Nxt platform. Based on such feedback, limitations of the current software have been identified.

One limitation for example is the need for all platform features to use the same token, i.e. the 'NXT' coin, not only for the payment of transaction fees to the network, but also for most transactions that need to use some token to measure value, e.g. pricing of asset exchange ask/bid orders, prices of digital goods listed on the marketplace, exchange rates of monetary system currencies. For many business needs, a custom blockchain is desired, with its own payment token, which can currently be provided by the Nxt platform only by means of offering a 'clone' - i.e., a completely separate blockchain, running a modified version of the same software, but not linked in any other way to the original Nxt blockchain.

The disadvantage of this solution is that a business which needs such a clone blockchain must run its own servers, generating blocks and processing transactions. In addition to being a burden for most small businesses, running a blockchain on only a few servers with few accounts creating blocks ('forging') lowers the system security, as compared to the main public Nxt blockchain currently running on hundreds of servers with many independent forging accounts. Such a clone also is bound to lag behind the current public chain software, in terms of feature additions and security bug fixes.

Another limitation of the current design, which is common to all other blockchain platforms too, is the so-called 'blockchain bloat'. This occurs because every node needs to store all transactions ever created since the blockchain was started, and not only store them, but re-process all of them when it downloads the blockchain for the first time. This is a security requirement stemming from the trustless design of blockchain platforms.

Being a proof-of-stake cryptocurrency, the balance of an account ('stake') at a given blockchain height determines, in a pseudo-random manner, whether this account is eligible to generate ('forge') the next block. For a node downloading the blockchain from scratch, the only way to verify that the next block it is downloading was indeed generated by a legitimate account (i.e. having sufficient stake), is to make sure it calculates and verifies each account balance as it downloads the blockchain, by processing all old transactions it encounters during the download. This represents a processing bottleneck that will only get worse as the blockchain size and the number of transactions per second increase.

While at the current transaction processing rate, bloat is not yet a problem, and we have come up with several innovative solutions to reduce it even more (such as prunable data - allowing optional removal of data from the blockchain, yet when needed automatically restoring such data in a trustless manner from archival nodes), bloat is a serious issue that must be solved in a fundamental way, in order for a blockchain platform to be future-proof and scalable".

~ Jean-Luc

And so, after 6 months of brainstorming, the development team had come up with the proposed solution: splitting NXT into a main chain used for consensus creation only, and multiple prunable childchains that keep separate ledgers of transactions, each child-chain using its own coin/token.

Ecosystem forks

"Nxt stand for innovation, good work".

~ superresistant

"Wow, I have to let this sink for a while. This is a huge change. I can see the benefits of it".

~ Tosch

In the SuperNET Slack a vigorous discussion immediately ensued and so, jl777 made an appearance, explaining the effect that the proposed changes would have on the market. According to his analysis, all asset holders would be doomed unless Ardor was stopped. He made a return to the nxtforum[22], concluding:

"I [have] stated that as long as NXT didn't break the way assets work that there was no reason to change from the NXT as the financial platform. [Ardor] model breaks the way assets work. The primary issue

---

22 https://nxtforum.org/core-development-discussion/nxt-2-0-design/msg210247

is that assets will be using NXT as the reference currency.

If a stock does a 2:1 split, the price is automatically adjusted so everyone ends up with the same value. In the upcoming Ardor:NXT split, there is no such mechanism, all asset will immediately lose half their value. (...)

1 + 1 = 2
delta / (1 - delta)

This is all the math you need, addition and division. There is no magic. (...)

I am speaking as a businessman, investor and asset issuer. Areas that I have proven skills in, but it probably doesn't matter that I understand business, financing, and issuing assets. I also had proven skills in the tech side and all my warnings about the API issues were ignored.

However in the asset area I created more asset values than everybody else combined for quite a while and that includes not just NXT but all decentralized platforms. And I did that in a span of just over a year. A big FUD storm against me and SuperNET pushed the price of it below

the value of just the core coins it held, wiping out all the gains. So I was reluctant to say anything due to the 'shoot the messenger' thing that happened last time. I have been silent, but when this farce of community 'feedback' is making it clear that it has already been decided by fiat that NXT will be massively devalued permanently, I decided to make an appearance directly. (...)

My biggest priority is to protect the millions of dollars invested into my assets. Since the NXT is apparently unconcerned about what the effects of totally changing the financial scope of the reference currency would do to everybody who built on top of it, I will have to take proactive steps to do so.

I will protect investors in my assets and unless there is a believable plan that protects asset holders' interests against the issues I raise in this post and any other that might arise, then my hand will be forced. Do not bother trying to convince me to compromise as I do not have the power to just let half the investors value get 'temporarily' pushed down by 50% without any clear path to recoup it. If you want to prevent this migration, you need to prevent Ardor and I have ZERO influence over that. I couldn't even get small API change reversed.

If indeed this Ardor plan moves forward without any protections to asset holders, there will be a way to transition off of the NXT blockchain to where it can be priced and traded against BTC and other currencies.

~ jl777

"Assets will be global. SuperBTC should become a token for a child chain instead of the asset that it is now. As it is pegged to BTC, it is a different economy, with its own risks.

An asset should be possible to trade in NXT, or in SuperBTC, by submitting the ask/bid transaction on the corresponding child chain, unless the asset issuer or the child chain properties do not allow that. Whether a specific asset is hidden or not accessible on some child chain, and if such restriction is permanent or can be changed, those are details that can be decided later".

~ Jean-Luc

"[Nxt 2.0] allows you to prune the existing NXT blockchain to the bare minimum. Think about it, we'll no longer need to store forever every message sent between two random users, every asset trade, every dividend payment of 0.002 NXT. We just save the state and proof that it is correct. We are developing blockchain technology which can scale to global scale."

~ Riker

The Nxt and the SuperNET projects had strong leaders, but with differing visions and working methods, and it was one too many to continue in collaboration. The early Nxt community gave jl777 their trust, help and money so he could create his grand project, and jl777 gave new users, more transactions and hype for the AE back. But as it became clear that the development of Nxt 2.0 would proceed as planned, he slammed the door, pointing out that the Nxt devs were forcing him to leave, and asked the moderators of the Nxtforum to block his forum account. Following in his footsteps was Sasha (nxtforum name: Coinomat)[23], an asset issuer, exchange owner, exchange bot programmer and long time Nxt supporter (now also a 'SuperNET service partner'). As he left, he announced an escape route, his new project, a Nxt-inspired asset platform to

---

[23] https://nxtforum.org/general-discussion/protocol-for-new-feature-implementation-and-significant-changes-in-nxt-core

which he would move all his assets when the platform had been developed (for this he raised 16 million USD in Bitcoins in its IPO[24]).

In a SuperNet Slack channel, jl777 admitted that moving the Super-NET tech to his own coin instead of Nxt had actually been his plan all along. The current situation with Nxt would just make it happen sooner rather than later. And so, in a „Declaration of Independence"[25], he plumped for an „Atomic Cross Chain Asset Standard", to save asset investors from being crushed by Nxt's "hardfork attacks".

Jean-Luc and the Nxt core development team had their reasons for changing the Nxt software code, and jl777 and Sasha surely had theirs for making a new start independently of Nxt. But no matter whom you supported, or were invested in, the public clash, the drama and consequent uncertainty that followed, was saddening and hurt both projects.

As Sasha left, his fiat-pegged assets NxtUSD and NxtEUR stopped working without prior notice and his assets Coinomat, cryptocard, IndexRev, Bitfirm and Cryptofund stopped paying dividends, leaving behind him only unfulfilled promises, a crashed asset market and investors in rage on the nxtforum[26]. In essence, nothing really changed for jl777's asset holders, except that investing in jl777 and SuperNET was NOT an investment in Nxt Services anymore. His assets had never paid dividends, except for NxtVenture, which jl777 'parked' until further notice. But leaving Nxt and nxtforum (and

24 https://bitcointalk.org/index.php?topic=1387944.0
25 https://bitcointalk.org/index.php?topic=1372879.0
26 https://nxtforum.org/cryptoasset-fund-projects/(ann)-coinomat-com/780

thereby all his asset threads) for good, meant further dumps of his assets despite his ever growing open source c codebase on github. Many Nxters felt scammed. And in the SuperNET camp, the community was angry with Nxt too. Some people just left both projects.

In real life, even if it is lived on the Internet, it is not the case that some are always right on everything while their antagonists are always wrong. No matter how long you spend looking for one truth, in life or in old threads and chats. And believe me, I've been digging. Sometimes a divorce, as hurtful as it may be, is the only constructive way for both parties to move forward. We call that a fork. The community forked.

In limbo

"I will create 2.0, in collaboration with the other core devs, in the way we consider technically best, and we have already spent plenty of time discussing and refining the design before announcing it publicly. The community gets to decide whether to use it".

~ Jean Luc[27]

HAD Nxt become centralised through development? What if Jean-Luc made new incompatible changes to the core code in the near future? Nxt 1.0 was working perfectly, why even change it? It scared investors and made external programmers afraid to rely on the Nxt API[28]. And without a clear and convincing roadmap for Nxt 2.0, not

27 https://nxtforum.org/core-development-discussion/nxt-2-0-design/msg 210387
28 https://bitcointalk.org/index.php?topic=1375670.0

even long time Nxters from the community could wholeheartedly argue that Jean-Luc had made the optimal decision on behalf of Nxt. What was the core development team's exact plan? Several competitors had emerged and gained magnificent market cap from ICO funding rounds, giving them millions of dollars for development and marketing.... BCNext had raised only 21 Bitcoins back in 2013, and besides that the Nxt platform already included the features that most other projects were raising money to develop. How were we to be competitive in marketing Nxt 2.0, and how were we to raise money for Nxt's further development?

On May 23, 2016, the announcement of "Ardor" put an end to the speculation.

NXT

2.0; ardor

NXT Cryptocurrency

NXT 2.0; ARDOR

Written by: apenzl, Jean-Luc

May 23, 2016, 06:08:56 pm:

> *"Announcing Ardor (Nxt 2.0), the successor to the pioneering Nxt platform, which has been an inspiration for many other successful blockchain projects".*
>
> ~ Jean-Luc, lead developer of Nxt[1]

Nxt 2.0 will not be a fork of the Nxt blockchain. Nxters are to keep their NXT tokens and can continue to use the Nxt 1.0 platform. Ardor is to be released on public net in Q2/Q3, 2017, but the core development team are committed to continue providing support for the Nxt 1.0 platform for at least one year after the Ardor launch.

Developers working with Nxt 1.0 (NRS 1.9 or a later release) can feel safe that their code will keep working on the Nxt 1.0 branch, and, if they want to do so after Ardor has been launched, they can port their projects to an Ardor childchain[2]. The Core Team will provide help and support for users that wish to move their enterprises from Nxt 1.0 to an Ardor childchain.

---

1 https://nxtforum.org/core-development-announcements/nxt-2-0-overview
2 One exception, as announced on its release, is the Nxt add-ons feature (available for developers from Nxt 1.8.0e), as this will undergo significant refactoring in 2.0. "Keep any custom add-on code simple, and be prepared to have to change it for 2.0 or discard it", lead developer Jean-Luc writes. Source: https://nxtforum.org/nrs-releases/nrs-v1-8-0e. You can follow the Nxt development in nxtforum.org, if you're in doubt about anything, or want to contribute the Nxt/Ardor project, contact the core developers.

„The architecture of the next-generation Nxt platform, Nxt 2.0, will take the system further, provide scalability, make it even more flexible, yet preserve its security and stability.

The fundamental concept of the Nxt 2.0 design is a clean separation of „forging token" and „transactional token". A separation of these two functions is what we believe can achieve both much greater scalability, by reducing blockchain bloat, and flexibility, by allowing multiple other transactional tokens to be used, in effect allowing custom „child chains" to exist and run on the same network of nodes.

This new flexible architecture allows users to create their own blockchains, customised to fit their needs, while drawing security from the collective ecosystem of the global Nxt 2.0 platform.

Gains and benefits

The scalability benefit should be obvious. A new node downloading the blockchain only needs to download and process the transactions from the forging chain, and the latest state snapshot. No validation and processing of any old child chain transactions will be needed, resulting in huge performance gains and storage space savings. Old transactions from all child chains can be pruned, and kept only on archival nodes, which in the future can specialize as commercial service providers, to provide this archival function for a fee, yet in a trustless way.

Each child chain will have its own native transactional token, which will have independent market value, or could be pegged by the child chain creator to an external unit of value (e.g. BTC, a fiat currency, or some other asset).

In a transparent way, this makes it possible to conduct transactions denominated in the transaction sender's token of choice, by just designating the transaction to belong to the specific child chain available for that token. For example, assets can be traded not only for NXT, but for BTC or EUR, as long as such a child chain with a token pegged to that currency exists. Digital goods listed on a specific child chain automatically have their prices denominated in that chain token, and so on.

As transactions on each child chain pay fees in their native token, users of a specific child chain do not need to acquire and deal with NXT coins only to pay fees. End users do not even need to be aware of the existence of the forging chain which takes fees in NXT only. A child chain creator can sponsor their chain, by covering fees for the users, even for a token that otherwise does not have a market value.

Since all child chains are run by the same code, they all can support the same features (transaction types), and at launch those will be all the features of the current Nxt platform. But a chain can optionally be limited to support only a subset of the globally available transaction types, thus excluding features that are not needed by the specific child chain creator business, are undesirable, or have legal restrictions in their jurisdiction.

Child chains can enforce further rules on transactions denominated in their token, such as permissioning, limiting which accounts are authori-

zed to issue specific transaction types, in order to e.g. comply with KYC rules for a child chain pegged to a fiat currency, or assets marketed to a jurisdiction imposing additional restrictions on who can trade them.

Even though they have their own tokens, all child chains will gain security from the fact that all nodes validate all transactions on all chains. As there is no forging on child chains themselves, it doesn't matter if a child chain has only a few active users and not many transactions per day. It will be fully secured by the vast network of nodes running the global Nxt platform. A small business that needs a blockchain no longer needs to run their own servers and forging nodes. The forging chain guarantees security for all child chains, and collects fees from them. In return, each of the child chains gets the ability to be pruned. Child chains no longer need to keep all their old data going back to genesis in order to be secure, because they do not forge.

Since all nodes run the same software, new features, bugfixes, and security patches, will be automatically available to all child chains. This is a significant improvement over the current cloned private blockchain solution, which requires custom software for each chain, that can easily get out of date and out of sync with the main Nxt platform.

~ Jean-Luc, lead developer of Nxt[3]

Distribution of coins

"The Core Developers recognise the tremendous contributions of the investors and holders of the original Nxt 1.0, without whom

---

3 Source: https://nxtforum.org/core-development-announcements/nxt-2-0-overview

Ardor would not be possible, and have decided to grant them exclusive rights to the new tokens.

There will initially be two distributions of tokens: one for the main chain token (Ardor), and one for the token for the first child chain to be launched (IGNIS)".

~ Jean-Luc

NXT holders will get Ardor tokens 1:1, based on the average of NXT in their accounts during a 3 months' snapshot period, beginning July 14, 2016, and ending 3 months later, on October 13, at block height 1000000. In addition to this, a final snapshot of the Nxt 1.0 ledger will be taken at the time of the Ardor Genesis block creation.

Anyone holding NXT in their account at that time will be credited IGNIS-tokens at least 1 : 0.5. The remaining ~50% of IGNIS-tokens will be allocated for funding of the development team, business development and other operations that need funding to make the Nxt 2.0 project a success.

ARDOR - The Descendant of Nxt

"Nxt is in the process of giving financial power back to the people. With this power in their hands, who knows what will be created next".

~ Jones

More than a few Q&A's were held, core developers sitting on one side and stakeholders, external developers, the Nxt Community on the other. As the details sunk in, it was as if new life was being breathed into Nxt. Also, the work behind-the-scenes from TNSSE / Nxt Foundation began to show results, new investors and Nxters joined the ecosystem, and the NXT market cap started rising dramatically.

Besides all the Nxt features described in this book, some of the new features to come with the Ardor platform are:

1. **Blockchain as a Service** - Ardor will open blockchain development to organizations and individuals across the world. The high barriers to getting started with Blockchain are about to vanish. Anyone will be able to create their own solutions using the blockchain technology with the Ardor child chains. From single users all the way up to FinTech startups and governments, create their own child chain and interact with the whole blockchain ecosystem.

2. **Manageable Blockchain Size** - Ardor will solve the problem of scalability by separating transactions and data that do not affect security from those that do, and moving all of those that don't affect security onto child chains. The Ardor team will create the first child chain to house many Nxt 1.0 tools as well as future features. This small size also comes with short transaction times so processes need only a fraction of time compared to Bitcoin to execute functions.

3. **A Decentralized Asset Exchange** - based on the Nxt Asset Exchange, Ardor will provide users with the ability to trade assets on

any child chain for any of the child chain tokens. This allows child chains to interact with each other and opens up numerous opportunities for collaboration as well as allow cross chain asset trading, a long-requested feature within the Nxt ecosystem.

4. Decentralized Voting and Governance Systems - Ardor will be at the core of decentralized consensus in the future. Secure and anonymous voting will be an available feature on all child chains as it is on the Nxt platform.

5. Phased Transactions - Users can set multiple conditions before a transaction is executed, such as a minimum number of votes and a set amount of time. Like Nxt, Ardor will use Smart Transactions. With this, users will only need to submit the parameters necessary for the transaction and the ID of the functionality they want to use. The transaction process is also completely decentralized. No centralized server, service, or application is needed.

"Rather than providing smart contracts, NXT is focused on implementing the important use cases and functions directly into the core of both Nxt and Ardor. This approach has proven to be scalable and secure and will become more so when Ardor is released."

~ Riker

The blockchain evolution is happening at a rapid pace. Nxt 1.0 inspired and paved the way for many blockchain 2.0 startups, and an increasing number of forward looking developers, corporations and governments are now finally looking into the technology.

With Ardor, the Nxt Team releases a fast and reliable Block-chain-of-Services, built on a well tested, well equipped and scalable financial platform. With advanced functionality which most other blockchain projects (however well funded) still only talk about or are only just beginning to develop, Nxt and Nxt 2.0 are likely to continue leading the way for many years to come - whether the work being done here will remain under the radar, as inspiration for others and used by Nxters only, is impossible to say. What can be said for sure though, is that Nxt already offers the most decen-tralised and advanced solution, and still remains a market leader in the space - by philosophy and technology if not by market cap. Blockchain technology is the new black and judging from the expo-nentially growing number of blockchain related google searches, we've still only seen the very beginning.

Implementation phases

Jean-Luc writes:

A. First, a system consisting of the forging chain and a few hardcoded child chains will be created. Each child chain will be using its own na-tive token, and child chain transactions will be bundled in ChildChain-Block transactions on the forging chain. However, while future pruning of those transactions will be possible, it will not be implemented for the time being, and as the system is just starting and total transaction count will be low, pruning will not yet be needed. Snapshot calculation and propagation will also not be implemented during this initial phase.

Since there is no pruning, all nodes will store all child chain data in this phase.

B. Next, pruning, snapshot calculation, and snapshot propagation will be implemented. It will be possible to prune child chain transactions, even retroactively in respect of those already created in phase A, because they will have been created as prunable by design. Each node will be storing the transactions of only the child chains the node owner is interested in, with archival nodes providing the service of making old transactions available for download by others. Child chain creation will still be a manual process.

C. Full automation of the child chain creation lifecycle. Users will be able to create their own child chains, without depending on the Nxt core development team. At this stage, we will have a much better understanding of the actual needs of child chain creators, the resources a child chain consumes and parameters it needs defined, and thus will be able to automate the process by adding the required transaction types to make it all self-service.

D. Advanced concepts of the so-called 'transparent forging' design can be put in place, allowing reduction of block times and increase of transaction processing throughput based on prediction of next forger, penalty for forgers missing their turn to forge, sending of transactions directly to the forging hub of the next forger, 'economic clustering' by marking of transactions with the block id of a recent block, and so on. Many of these potential improvements are only needed when there is a demand for high transaction processing capacity, but this demand can be satisfied only after the scalability and bloat reduction features have been provided by the prunable child chain design in the previous phases.

The precise ordering of those implementation steps is subject to change and adjustment, e.g. whether automating the lifecycle of child chain creation (phase C), or pruning and snapshot propagation (phase B) should be done first, will be decided depending on actual market needs after phase A has been achieved.

The full rollout of the proposed 2.0 design does not need to happen all in a single step, but as common in large software projects can be implemented in several phases.

Coding Ardor will take time. The Core Team does not want to launch an overhyped and half-finished system, but wants to make sure the new platform holds up to the high standards you have come to expect from Nxt 1.0. We consider this to be the de-facto reference standard of stability and performance that a blockchain platform should adhere to.

And so it goes. New chapters of this intense and fast-moving adventure are being continuously written with code, as transactions on the blockchain, confirmed by nodes in the wild, documented and pushed forward by a decentralised community of supporters of Nxt.

Implementation details can be found here:

https://nxtforum.org/core-development-announcements/nxt-2-0-overview

You can find an outline on how each Nxt feature will be ported to IGNIS here:

https://nxtforum.org/core-development-announcements/announcing-nxt-2-0-roadmap

Damelon on June 19, 2016, 09:21:30 pm[4]:

Just received this out of the blue...

Address: 1BCN1ugdKdWd9pQ8Am9hMhtHZfmbXzxE8a
Message: I am glad to see that Nxt keeps evolving. Good luck!
Signature: G8b5ou0qstF8Mo6LM74NSL+73/YIMkk4cVRjeNz5sKQ1dAIAZ-
dhj43bQJJH1392+ybGTYa63kb1BHO9TbPDFXho=

For those who do not recognise this address, this is a message from BCNext, who originally created Nxt.

---

 4 https://nxtforum.org/core-development-announcements/(ann)-ardor-or-nxt-2-0-a-scalable-child-chain-platform/msg219417

NXT

plugins

NXT Cryptocurrency

NXT PLUGINS

Written by: apenzl

The plug-in system is an example of the philosophy of flexibili-ty and versatility that is at the heart of Nxt. Nxt Plugins enables third-party software developers to add functionality to the Nxt client.

To make it secure to use plugins, the Nxt Client lets you log in to accounts without entering your passphrase. If you need to send a transaction which requires you to enter your passphrase, you can click on „disable plugins". Or you can enable plugins for a certain account only, and disable them for others, so that you don't use plugins with accounts that holds big amounts of NXT.

Plugins are disabled in the client as default, but it is very easy to switch this in the settings.

Best practices

For developers:
1.   Use open source code.
2.   Reproducible packaging procedure.
3.   Package downloaded directly from the same source control system.
4.   Hash of the package posted on the nxtforum.org.
5.   Additional PGP or some form of digital signature which confirms the identity of the developer.

For users of Nxt Plugins:

1. Do not install plugins which do not rely on the distribution system described above.
2. Use only plugins installed by yourself, avoid using plugins when connecting to a public node.
3. Do not use plugins when connecting to an account which has a significant amount of NXT.
4. Make sure a plugin uses only JavaScript and Html, avoid plugins which rely on 'fat client' technologies such as Java Applet, ActiveX, Flash etc., in other words do not confirm any browser security prompt when using plugins.
5. Do not follow links from plugin pages to external websites.

Another way to make sure that a plugin is secure is to only download your plugins from https://nxtplugins.com. Plugins offered on NxtPlugins.com have been reviewed by expert developers. Nxt-Plugins.com lists plugins on the NxtPlugins.com site and directly on the Nxt Marketplace. Purchase deliveries happen automatically. Every feedback from the blockchain is shown and it enables a rating for a plugin after a purchase has been made.

Nxt Plugin examples

Slackchat[1]

Lets you chat in Nxtchat.slack directly from the Nxt client UI.

---

1 https://github.com/valortech/slackchat, https://nxtforum.org/nxt-plugins/slackchat-plugin. There is also a "simplechat" plugin available on the git repo, made available for future chat-app implementers so they don't have to bootstrap another chat style plugin from scratch.

Shapeshift[2]

Lets you exchange NXT with other cryptocurrencies directly from within the Nxt Client, without any registration, using the ShapeShift instant exchange.

Filesharing[3]

Upload a .torrent file or a magnet link to the blockchain as prunable data, which is searchable in the blockchain by name and description, and classifiable using tags (keywords). Check whether a torrent is a known fake with the integrated FakeSkan[4].

Dividend Scanner[5]

Check dividends and ordinary payments you receive from your assets paying dividends. The plugin shows you the distribution of your assets as well as the distribution of your income.

NXT / asset Dividend Payout[6]

Allows you to send dividends via normal transactions and exclude certain accounts (issuer, escrow). You can send either NXT or assets and you can attach a message. The message attached to the transaction is prunable to keep the cost down.

2 https://bitbucket.org/lyaffe/shape_shift/overview,
https://nxtforum.org/nxt-plugins/shapeshift-integration-plugin
3 https://github.com/toenu23/nxt-filesharing
https://nxtforum.org/general-discussion/(preview)-torrents-plugin
4 https://bitsnoop.com/info/about.html
5 https://nxtplugins.com/index.php?details&id=2
6 https://nxtplugins.com/index.php?details&id=10

Quack Atomic Swap[7]

Quack enables easy, safe and secure atomic swaps of Nxt-based Assets and Currencies. With Quack, Nxt users can directly exchange Assets, Currencies or NXT with no counterparty risk. Directly exchange Asset<>Asset, Asset<>Currency, or Currency<>Currency, swapping them directly without the need to convert to NXT. Multiple swaps supported in a single session. Blockchain based. No off-chain communication required.

Add your own

Developers interested in making Nxt Services can get an introduction to coding for blockchains and using the Nxt API at nxter.org/developers, or sign up to nxtforum.org or nxtchat.slack, to interact with other active devs, be it core - or 3rd party Nxt developers.

7 https://nxtplugins.com/index.php?details&id=9,
https://nxtforum.org/general-discussion/quack-nxt-atomic-asset-swap

Fiat is Failing

let battle commence?

 **NXT** Cryptocurrency

FIAT IS FAILING.
LET BATTLE COMMENCE?

Written by: Robert Bold

Cryptocurrency[1] has now reached such an advanced stage of technological development that it would be remarkable if there was a national government anywhere in the world that was still not yet paying it serious attention; at the same time, the debt based fiat monetary system, following the 'global' financial crisis of 2007/8[2], remains in a critical condition[3].

---

1 'Cryptocurrencies [which are a type of digital currency] typically feature decentralized control (as opposed to a centralized electronic money system, such as PayPal) and a public ledger (such as bitcoin's block chain) which records transactions.' Source: http://en.wikipedia.org/wiki/Cryptocurrency
'Cryptocurrencies are designed to be capable of replacing cash...No central power has arbitrary control over the money supply.'
Source: https://bitcoinmagazine.com/15862/digital-vs-virtual-currencies/
Cryptocurrency 1.0: decentralised, P2P, cryptographically secured, digital payment systems.
Cryptocurrency 2.0: '...is the application of blockchain or distributed ledger technology to things other than digital currency. The block chain offers the ability to facilitate decentralized ownership and store, transfer and process information in a decentralized, programmable way. Many consider that innovation to be the true value of this technology.'
Source: http://www.coindesk.com/crypto-2-0-roundup-bitcoins-revolution-moves-beyond-currency.
2 'While the housing and credit bubbles [the immediate causes of the financial crisis] were building, a series of factors caused the financial system to both expand and become increasingly fragile, a process called financialization.' Source: http://en.wikipedia.org/wiki/Financial_crisis_of_2007%E2%80%9308
3 Is the debt based fiat monetary creation and allocation system sufficiently robust to be able to respond adequately to the 'extraordinary' demands that are being placed on it?
'...extraordinary central bank action has become the new normal in the developed world.
Faced with the twins threats of deflation and economic stagnation, monetary policymakers are reaching for their interest rate levers and digital money-printing tools in a bid to stave off recessions and debt deflationary dynamics.'
Source: http://www.telegraph.co.uk/finance/economics/11378193/How-central-banks-have-lost-control-of-the-world.html

What exactly the world's financial and monetary systems will look like beyond the short time horizon of the foreseeable future is impossible to know but we can at least be sure that the powerful private vested interests (primarily the commercial banks) who support the fiat monetary system in its present form will seek to preserve it substantially unchanged as far as possible and for as long as possible (a subject which is discussed in more detail in the forthcoming second article in the series: 'Is fiat a fraud? From false commodity to false economy').

Has war been declared and, if so, where are the battle lines?

As yet there has been no internationally co-ordinated government level response to the disruptive potential of decentralised ledger technology (i.e. cryptocurrency 1.0 and 2.0), although work is currently being carried out which will ultimately lead to a response at the European Union level specifically regarding investments[4].

---

4 On 22 April 2015, The European Securities and Markets Authority (equivalent to the Securities and Exchange Commission in the US) issued a call for evidence regarding 'Investment using virtual [sic] currency or distributed ledger technology'.
Source: https://www.finextra.com/finextra-downloads/newsdocs/esma_call_for_evidence.pdf
ESMA states on its website that it:
'...is interested in how different virtual currencies and the associated blockchain, or distributed ledger, can be used in investments. There are now facilities available to use the blockchain infrastructure as a means of issuing, transacting in and transferring ownership of securities in a way that bypasses the traditional infrastructure for public offer and issuance of securities, trading venues like exchanges and central securities depositaries or other typical means of recording ownership. ESMA would like to find out more about these market developments and in particular to know to what extent the use of the blockchain could enter the financial mainstream, and how it could be used.'
Nxt is the example of the digital currency platform ESMA uses in its 'call for evidence' to illustrate how distributed ledger technology works.

In the meantime there has, to date, been a number of responses from individual countries, either specifically in respect of bitcoin or otherwise regarding all forms of digital currency, including for example:

- declaring the use of bitcoin as a parallel currency to be illegal (Russia).
- (whilst allowing citizens to buy or sell bitcoins amongst themselves), banning the country's banks from processing transactions involving bitcoin (China).
- stating (or at least intimating) that they do not recognise digital currencies as legal tender and therefore do not regulate them (Ireland).
- treating bitcoin as a commodity and banning its use as a currency (Japan).
- treating bitcoin as a foreign currency and banning its exchange with the national currency (Iceland).
- announcing the creation of a national digital currency and banning all others (Ecuador).
- regulating digital currencies to the extent of requiring 'digital currency businesses' to comply with anti-money laundering laws (Isle of Man).[5]
- announcing proposals to consult on how best to regulate digital

5 Digital currency businesses [as defined below] will have to comply with the Isle of Man's anti-money laundering (AML) laws from 1st April [2015] and will likely fall under the remit of the Financial Services Commission from the Summer.'
'[Those in] the business of issuing, transmitting, transferring, providing safe custody or storage of, administering, managing, lending, buying, selling, exchanging or otherwise trading or intermediating convertible virtual currencies, including cryptocurrencies or similar concepts where the concept is accepted by persons as a means of payment for goods or services, a unit of account, a store of value or a commodity.'
Source: http://www.coindesk.com/isle-of-man-introduces-regulation-for-bitcoin-businesses

currencies and in the meantime issuing guidance regarding their status/treatment for tax purposes (the US and UK).

So, whilst some governments apparently see digital currencies as constituting an immediate, existential threat to their financial and monetary systems (even their national sovereignty)[6] others are for the time being more welcoming, at least as regards the potential for blockchain technology to confer a competitive advantage on their economies[7].

Financial and monetary stability is, quite rightly, of paramount importance to governments but, despite the growing body of evidence to the contrary, they still regard that stability as best being achieved by the continuation of a debt based, fiat money creation and allocation system run by profit-maximising private banks, ostensibly subject to central bank control.

Happily, there are signs that this inter-governmental consensus may perhaps finally be starting to break down:

---

6 'A senior Central Bank [of Ireland] official has warned that virtual and digital currencies have the potential to challenge the sovereignty of states.': http://www.rte.ie/news/business/2014/0703/628309-bitfin-conference
7 'Osborne looks to virtual currencies in bid to make UK world fintech capital': https://www.finextra.com/news/fullstory.aspx?newsitemid=26337
Further details regarding the UK government's attitude towards 'digital' currency is contained in two recently published reports: 'Digital Currencies – response to the call for information': https://www.gov.uk/government/uploads/system/uploads/attachment_data/file/414040/digital_currencies_response_to_call_for_information_final_changes.pdf and 'Banking for the 21st Century – driving competition and choice ': https://www.gov.uk/government/uploads/system/uploads/attachment_data/file/416097/Banking_for_the_21st_Century_17.03_19_40_FINAL.pdf
See also:
'Virtual Currency Schemes – a further analysis', European Central Bank, February 2015: https://www.ecb.europa.eu/pub/pdf/other/virtualcurrencyschemesen.pdf
'Cryptotechnologies, a major IT innovation and catalyst for change'. European Banking Authority, 11 May 2015: https://www.abe-eba.eu/downloads/knowledge-and-research/EBA_20150511_EBA_Cryptotechnologies_a_major_IT_innovation_v1_0.pdf

For more than half a century, Iceland has suffered from serious monetary problems including inflation, hyperinflation, devaluations, an asset bubble and ultimately the collapse of its banking sector in 2008.

Other countries have faced similar problems. Since 1970, bank crises have occurred 147 times in 114 countries causing serious reductions in output and increases in debt. Despite its frequent failures, the banking system has remained essentially unchanged and homogenous around the world....[a] necessary step toward monetary reform is to increase awareness of the drawbacks and risks of the present system and why reform is needed.

This report will hopefully serve as a useful source of information for the coming debate on the money creation process in Iceland and how it could be reformed to serve society better in the future.

Extract from the Preface to 'Monetary Reform ~ a Better Monetary System for Iceland'[8] (March 2015)

The solution to the debt based fiat money problem being proposed for Iceland is the Sovereign Money System[9]. How this potential solution, which is also being advocated by the Positive Money campaign[10], compares with Nxt will be discussed in the third article in the series ('Comparing the potential of sovereign/positive money and Nxt to solve the debt-based fiat money problem').

---

8 https://positivemoney.org/wp-content/uploads/2015/04/monetary-reform-Iceland.pdf
9 Sovereign Money System: this, in effect, nationalises money by giving the central bank the exclusive power to create money and parliament the power to allocate how the money is used; the government then spends/invests it into circulation.
10 http://www.positivemoney.org

Regardless of the success or otherwise of the Positive Money campaign or the Icelandic initiative, the existing fiat monetary system looks set to continue, fundamentally unchanged, in the rest of the world indefinitely, thanks partly to the entrenched network effect that the existing system enjoys, partly to the commercial vested interest of the disproportionately powerful commercial banks[11] and partly also to:

- the collective bureaucratic inertia of the 'four pillars' of global economic governance (the International Monetary Fund[12], the World Bank, the World Trade Organization, the Financial Stability Board of the G20[13]) and of the Bank for International Settlement;

---

11 'The network of global corporate control' Stefania Vitali, James B. Glattfelder, and Stefano Battiston published in the New Scientist Magazine 22 October 2011 (Issue no. 2835): http://arxiv.org/PS_cache/arxiv/pdf/1107/1107.5728v2.pdf
'An analysis of the relationships between 43,000 transnational corporations has identified a relatively small group of companies, mainly banks, with disproportionate power over the global economy.'
Source: https://www.newscientist.com/article/mg21228354.500-revealed--the-capitalist-network-that-runs-the-world
12 But see: 'IMF report from 2012 by Jaromir Benes and Michael Kumhof (https://www.imf.org/external/pubs/ft/wp/2012/wp12202.pdf). The focus of the study is the so-called Chicago plan of the 1930s which the authors have updated to fit into today's economy.
The basic idea is that banks should be required to have full coverage for money they lend. Under this proposal, banks would no longer be allowed to create new money in the form of credit in connection with their lending activities. Instead, the central bank should be solely responsible for all the creation of all forms of money, not just paper money and coins. The advantages of such a system, according to the authors, are a more balanced economy without the booms and busts of the current system, the elimination of bank runs, and a drastic reduction of both public and private debt. The authors rely on both economic theory and historical examples, and state that inflation, according to their calculations, would be very low.'
Source: http://en.wikipedia.org/wiki/The_Chicago_Plan_Revisited
13 It should be noted however that the chair of the policy development committee of the Financial Stability Board, Adair Turner, wrote in his foreword to 'Monetary Reform – a Better Monetary System for Iceland' (March 2015) that the efforts to make the existing financial system more stable: 'have still failed to address the fundamental issue – the ability of banks to create credit, money and purchasing power, and the instability which inevitably follows. As a result, the reforms agreed to date still leave the world dangerously vulnerable to future financial and economic instability.'
Source: https://positivemoney.org/wp-content/uploads/2015/04/monetary-reform-Iceland.pdf

- large parts of the financial press; and last, but by no means least,
- mainstream economic theorists[14].

To be as effective as possible in getting our message listened to with attention it's not enough for cryptocurrency advocates only to refer to the fact that the current fiat monetary creation and allocation system leads to socially and economically damaging results and that it remains in a critical condition, we must also demonstrate that we understand why it does so (topics which are examined in more detail in the next article in the series: 'Is fiat a fraud? From false commodity to false economy').

Six years after the launch of blockchain technology (in the initial form of Bitcoin), the commercial banks are becoming increasingly aware of the competitive threat which this rapidly developing technology poses to their business[15].

They understand that their long-established centralised system of financial networks based, as they are, on restricted access to

.

---

14 'Mainstream economists', those who subscribe to '…neoclassical equilibrium theory and assimilated Neokeynesianism, or to put it differently, American textbook standard economics…Mainstream economics for the most part rests on the assumption of neutrality of money…If one believes in neutrality of money, then of course dysfunctions of the money system are not an obvious subject of concern, despite all financial crises. As a consequence, most mainstream economists find it difficult to see why monetary reform might be of relevance.' Joseph Huber, http://www.sovereignmoney.eu/sovereign-money-in-critical-context
15 The banking industry is now organising conferences to consider questions such as: What is the future of money? Do you know what cryptocurrencies mean for your business and for the future of financial services? Are you leveraging [the] blockchain? Are these developments an opportunity or a threat for traditional financial services providers?
Source: SWIFT Business Forum London, 23 April 2015, https://www.swift.com/insights/events/past-events/swift-business-forum-london-2015

the APIs[16] on which they run is now being challenged by a rapidly developing and expanding decentralised system of financial networks based on open API access which, in effect, makes possible the democratisation of financial power worldwide.

The banks also understand that cryptocurrency technology does not just represent a competitive threat to their dominant position in the provision of financial services in general it also represents (at least in theory) an existential threat to their virtual monopoly position as money creators and allocators which came about purely as an accident of history.

It's hardly surprising therefore that most of the major banks are now working on blockchain solutions/strategies albeit that, under the mantra of Bitcoin is bad, blockchain is good they seem to be currently focusing their attention on trying to adopt/adapt the capacity of bitcoin's blockchain technology to store data and execute financial contracts without needing to use the reward mechanism of the bitcoin currency to secure the integrity of the ledger. Their objective appears to be the creation of a private, federated blockchain in which every hashing institution is known and trusted.

Whether that would work and, assuming it did, what effect, if any, it would have on the continuing development, implementation and rate of adoption of genuinely decentralised, trustless, mathemati-

---

16 An example of an API (Application Programming Interface) in the mainstream financial system is the VISA network's merchant API which only the merchant, as a trusted party, is allowed to program. Examples of APIs in cryptocurrency based systems include: the transaction scripting language, the P2P network protocol and the 'Northbound' client, all of which are open source and are therefore available for anyone to program.

cally secure, blockchain technologies, such as Nxt, remains to be seen.

Much more promising than private, federated blockchains (technologically speaking and also in terms of social utility) is the idea of hybrid systems that, in effect, bridge the gap between the banks' existing infrastructure and blockchain technology. A prime example being 44 Phones' hybrid cash and cryptocurrency platform[17] which has been developed as a mobile banking application using the Nxt blockchain technology to deliver mobile money via SMS, mobile app and the web.

Systems such as these may well prove to be the salvation of the fiat monetary system which otherwise left to its own devices seems set to go that one step further than it did in 2007/8 and irretrievably implode.

In the meantime, many cryptocurrency enthusiasts appear to welcome the prospect of a mainstream financial collapse believing that it would clear the way for cryptocurrency to take its rightful place in the world.

In practice, though, it is much more likely that in the event of such a collapse national governments would take emergency powers[18] and impose a top down solution designed in collaboration with,

---

17 'UK's 44 Phones Building Blockchain-Based International Mobile Network, Mobile Money Service.': http://allcoinsnews.com/2015/04/06/londons-44-phones-establishing-blockchain-based-mobile-network-poc-mobile-money-service
18 For example (in the UK) the Civil Contingencies Act 2004, Part 2 Emergency Powers, S. 22 (2) (h): http://www.legislation.gov.uk/ukpga/2004/36/pdfs/ukpga_20040036_en.pdf

and therefore favouring, the banking industry rather than adopting a solution from the genuinely free market, unless that solution had already achieved such widespread acceptance that public and commercial pressure to adopt it was irresistible (an unlikely scenario admittedly, but anything is possible).

Are we ready for war?

The short answer is no, we're not. At least not one against a common enemy. Instead, the cryptocurrency industry appears to be engaged in its own permanent civil war. Have a quick read of some of the discussion threads on bitcointalk.org and it soon becomes obvious that many, perhaps most, people involved in cryptocurrency seem to regard the only enemy as being the developers, owners and promoters of any cryptocurrency they don't currently own which is doing better than the ones they do.

What we must always bear in mind however is that the cryptocurrency industry is still in its infancy and until the various (competing) blockchain technologies become established and their real value gets priced by the market, the price and purchasing power of their native currencies will continue to be subject to much greater potential volatility than that of fiat currencies. In the longer term, of course, the reverse may well eventually turn out be the case.

Can war be avoided?

Answer: it depends if you listen to your heart or your head.

Emotionally speaking, war is inevitable and the 'enemy' is either other cryptos or fiat money or both (including their respective providers, users, supporters and fellow travellers), depending on what your unmediated instinct for self-preservation tells you. Strategically speaking, yes, war can be avoided as there shouldn't, in reality, be any enemy to fight, at least not as far as cryptocurrency is concerned.

To acknowledge someone as an 'enemy' is to acknowledge that instead of merely competing with them one wants, if possible, to destroy them in a 'zero-sum' fight to the death where the winner takes all and the loser ceases to exist.

However, there seems little possibility of blockchain technology on its own destroying the fiat based monetary system and absolutely no advantage to be gained by claiming that it could.

Moreover, other cryptocurrencies aren't the enemy either; no one single coin, not even Bitcoin itself, will be able to monopolize what will inevitably become an ever-expanding and diversifying market.

Every cryptocurrency that gains a foothold in the mainstream will help to educate the wider population about the benefits of the technology, thereby opening up the market for cryptocurrency usage more generally.

In my opinion, the language of war is not the most appropriate category of discourse to use in the ongoing struggle to establish cryptocurrency. Instead we should be more inclined to use the language of diplomacy in recognition of the fact that whatever 'best case' scenarios we might imagine for cryptocurrency, the financial landscape in which cryptocurrencies will be operating in the future will, in the absence of a complete and irretrievable global financial collapse, almost certainly continue to be dominated by the existing debt based fiat monetary system.

It may even be that cryptocurrencies, by strengthening local economies and thereby building greater resilience into national economies and ultimately the global economy, will actually help the existing fiat monetary system to survive and traditional banks to continue in business.

Seen in that light, it would actually be in the banks' own best interests to be more accommodating in their attitude towards independent cryptocurrencies and, for our part, perhaps we should be thinking of making a virtue out of the fact that cryptocurrency usage in the mainstream economy, if sufficiently widespread, could have the unintended consequence of actually bolstering the fiat monetary system.

NXT

additional resources

NXT Cryptocurrency

ADDITIONAL RESOURCES

Sites

https://nxt.org
https://nxter.org
https://nxtwiki.org

Nxt Clients

Mobile:
https://nxtwiki.org/wiki/Mobile_App

Full Nxt Client (NRS):
https://nxtforum.org/nrs-releases/
https://bitbucket.org/JeanLucPicard/nxt/downloads

MyNxt wallet:
https://wallet.mynxt.info

Supernet Lite wallet (MGW):
(for NRS, hit the 'advanced' button)
https://nxtforum.org/lite-multigateway-releases/

Blockchain explorers

https://mynxt.info
https://nxtportal.org

Nxt Community

https://nxtforum.org
https://nxtchat.slack.com
(sign up: https://nxtchat.herokuapp.com)

https://www.reddit.com/r/NXT

First Nxt thread ("The Firehose"):
https://bitcointalk.org/index.php?topic=345619.0
Official Nxt thread on bitcointalk.org:
https://bitcointalk.org/index.php?topic=587007.0

Contribute to NXTER.org:
https://nxter.org/get-published-get-paid-nxtp

Nxt Foundation

http://www.nxtfoundation.io

Jelurida

Private blockchain solutions
https://nxter.org/jelurida-qa-nxt-core-devs-mean-business/

For investors

https://nxter.org/exchange
https://nxter.org/assethub
https://coinmarketcap.com/currencies/nxt

For developers

http://localhost:6876/test
https://nxtwiki.org/wiki/Testnet

Nxt API:
https://nxtwiki.org/wiki/The_Nxt_API

Other resources:
https://nxter.org/developers

Nxt Peer Explorer:
http://www.peerexplorer.com

Nxt Whitepaper:
https://nxtwiki.org/wiki/Whitepaper:Nxt

Nxt Blockchain Tutorial:
https://nxtwiki.org/wiki/Nxt_Blockchain_Tutorial

Nxt open source code (GPL license):
https://nxtwiki.org/wiki/Nxt_Software_Change_Log

Dev mailing list:
http://nxt.org/cgi-bin/mailman/listinfo/nrs-development

Suggest improvements to Nxt:
https://nxtforum.org/nxt-improvement-proposals

ARDOR

https://ardorplatform.org
https://ardorhub.org
https://nxter.org/ardor-blockchain

Ardor on bitcointalk.org:
https://bitcointalk.org/index.php?topic=1518497.0